# THIS BOOK BELONGS TO

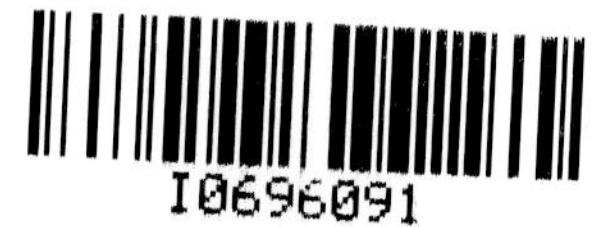



.........................................................

.........................................................

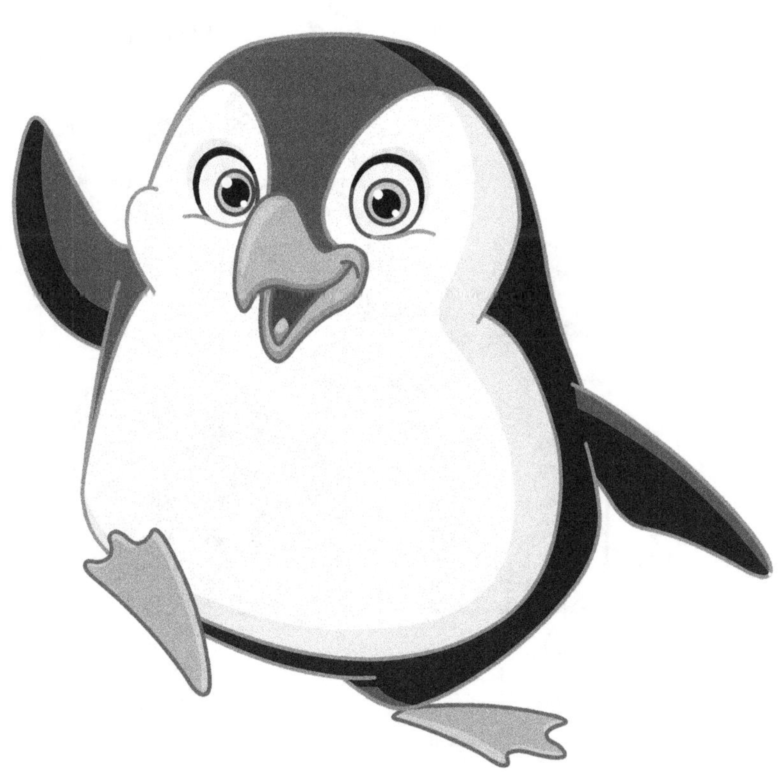

# Penguin
# Coloring Book

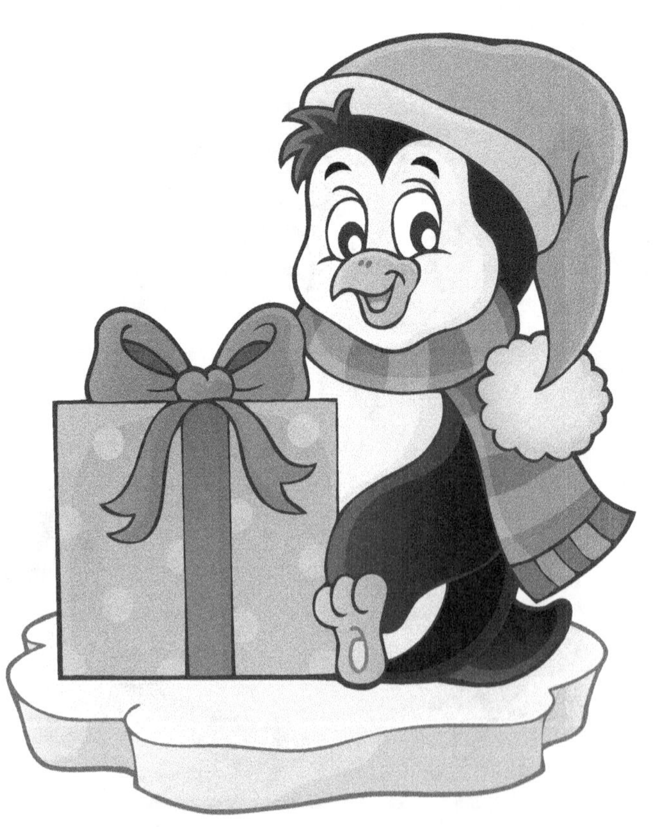

# Test Your Colour

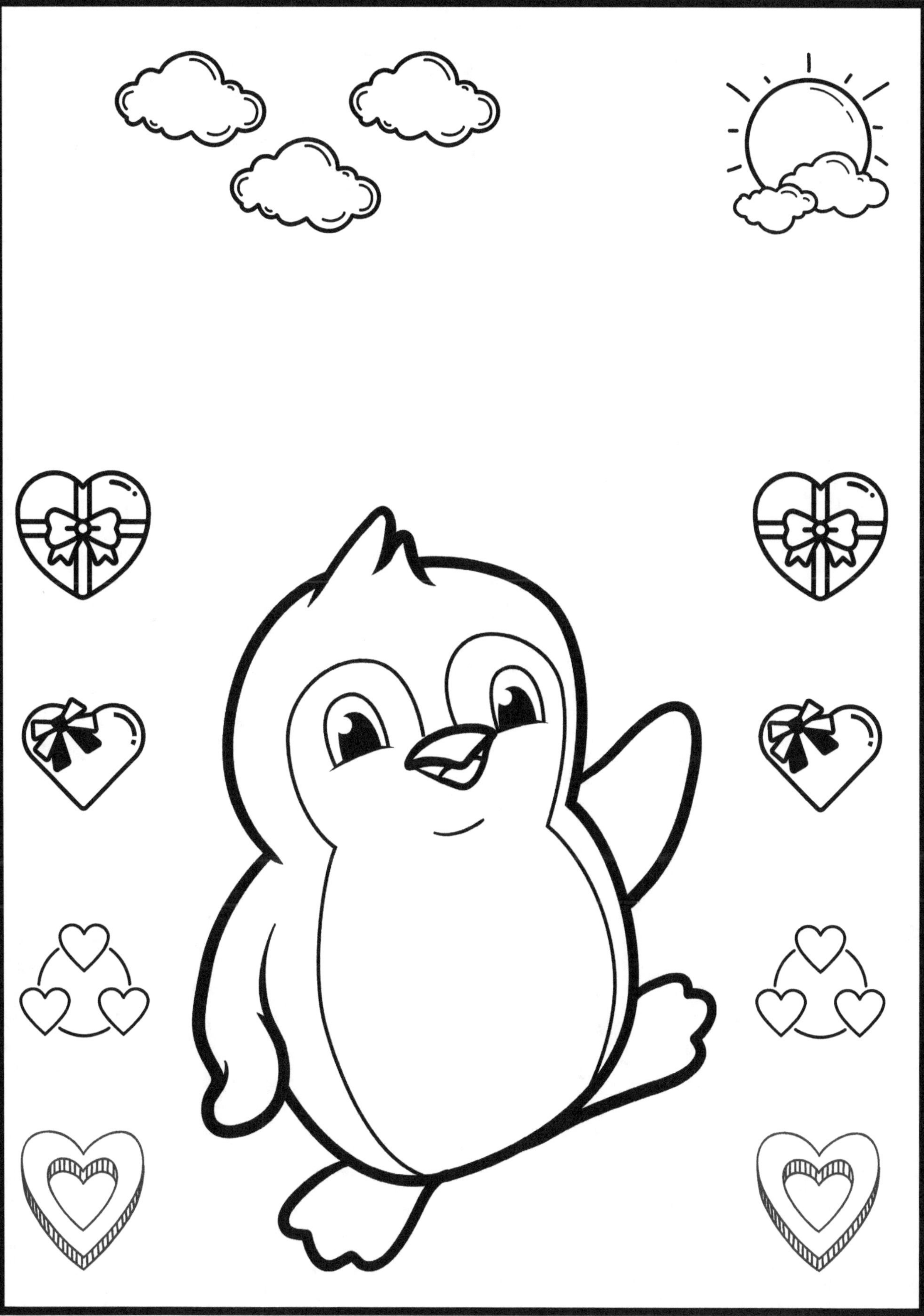

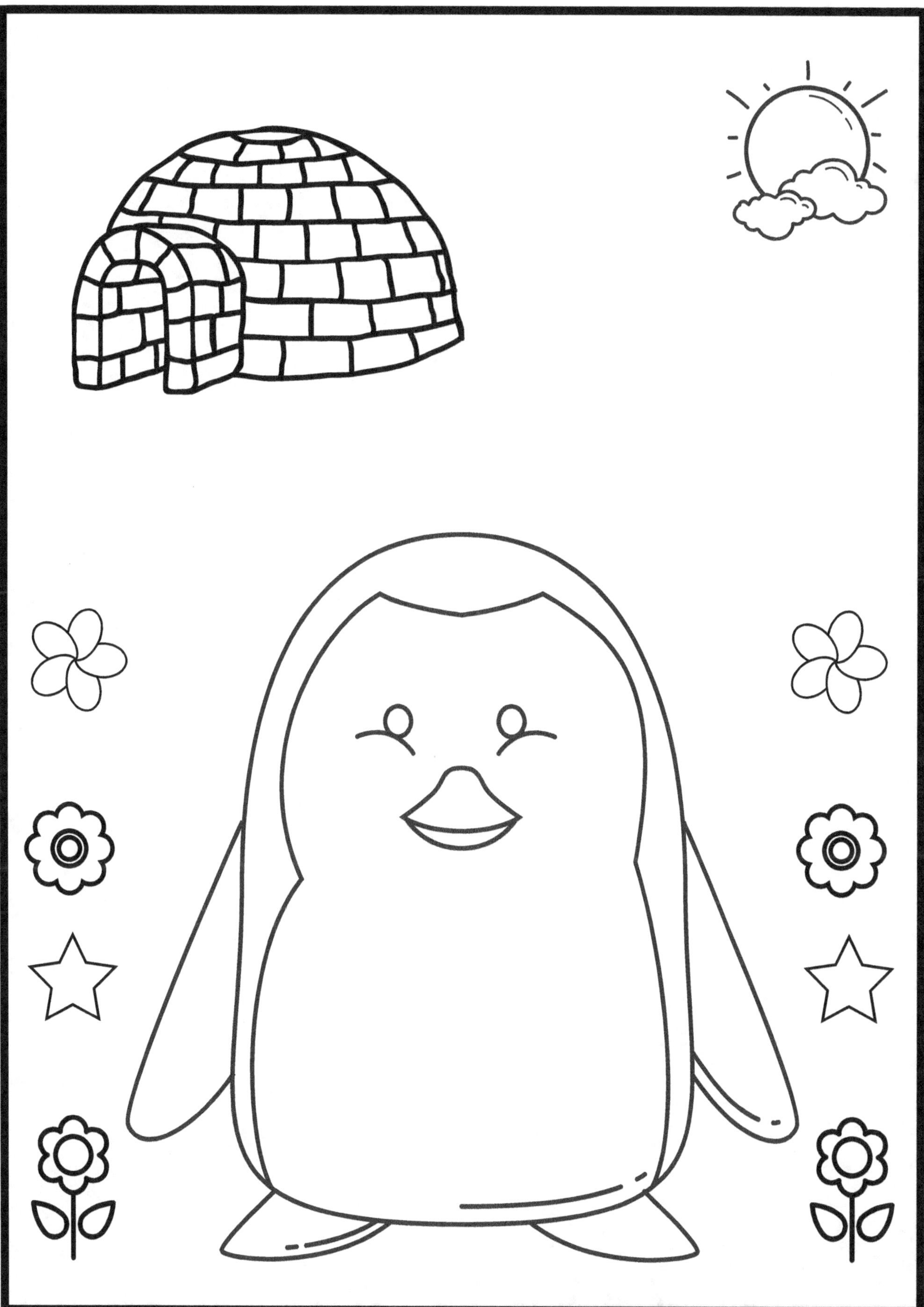

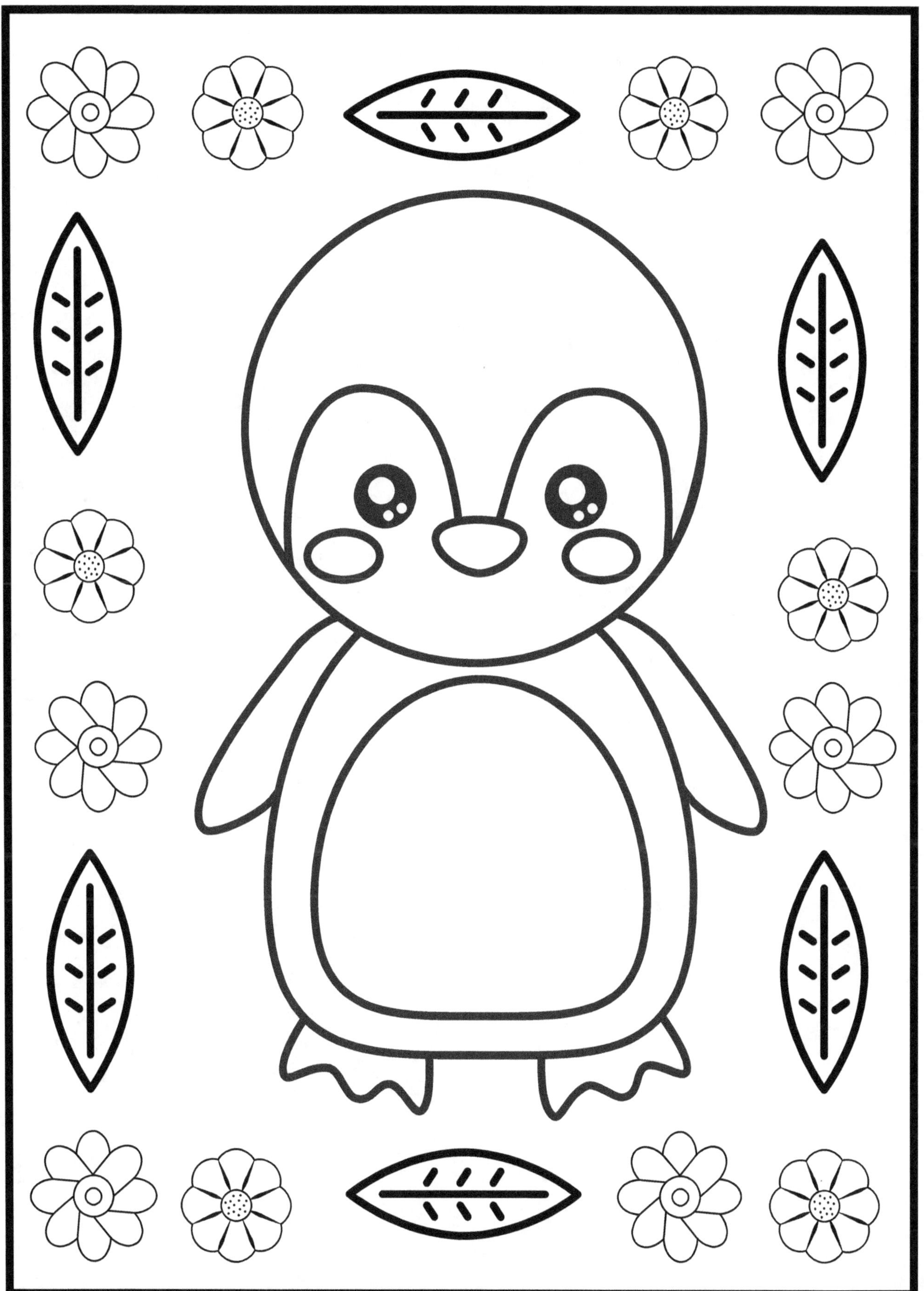

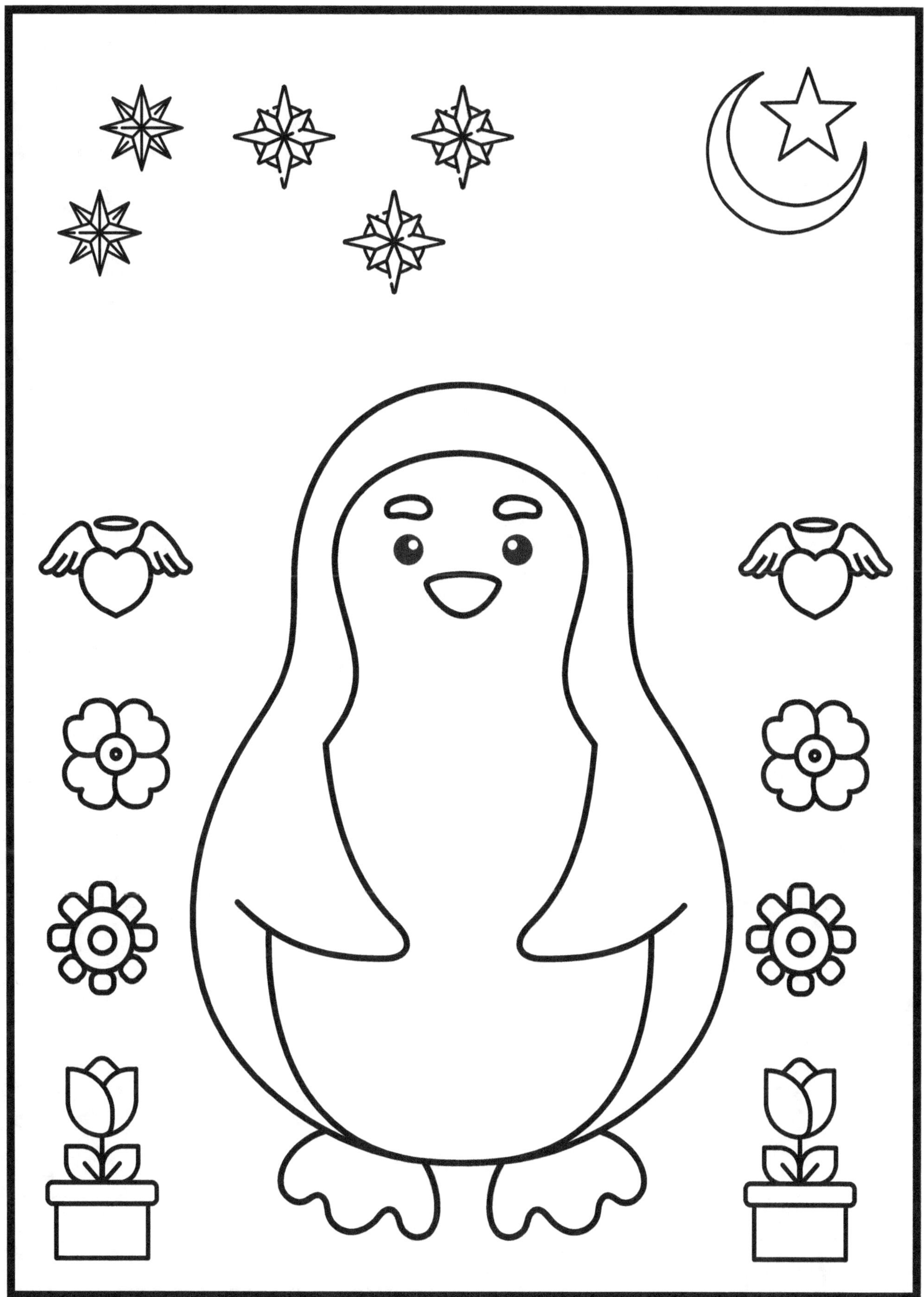

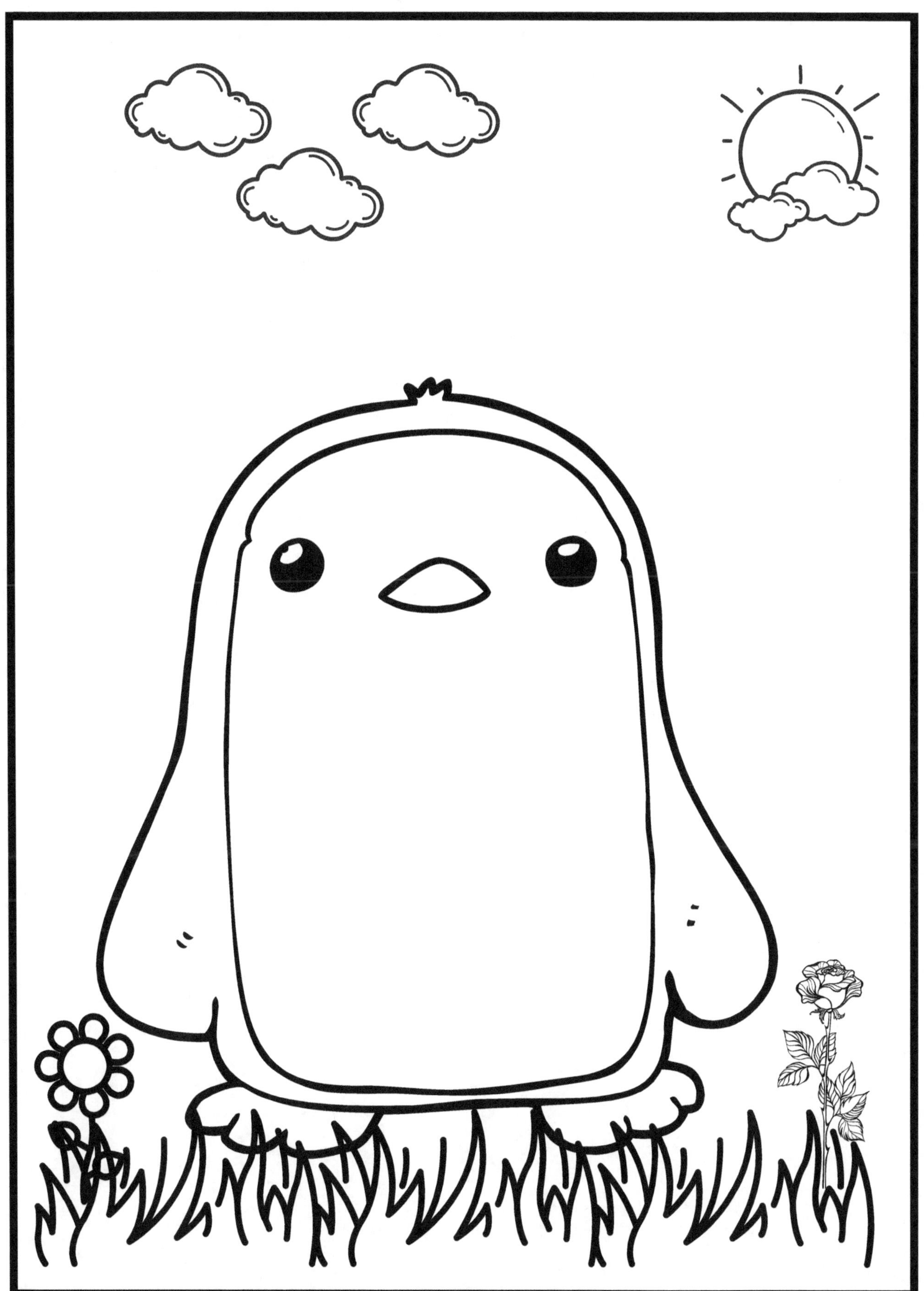

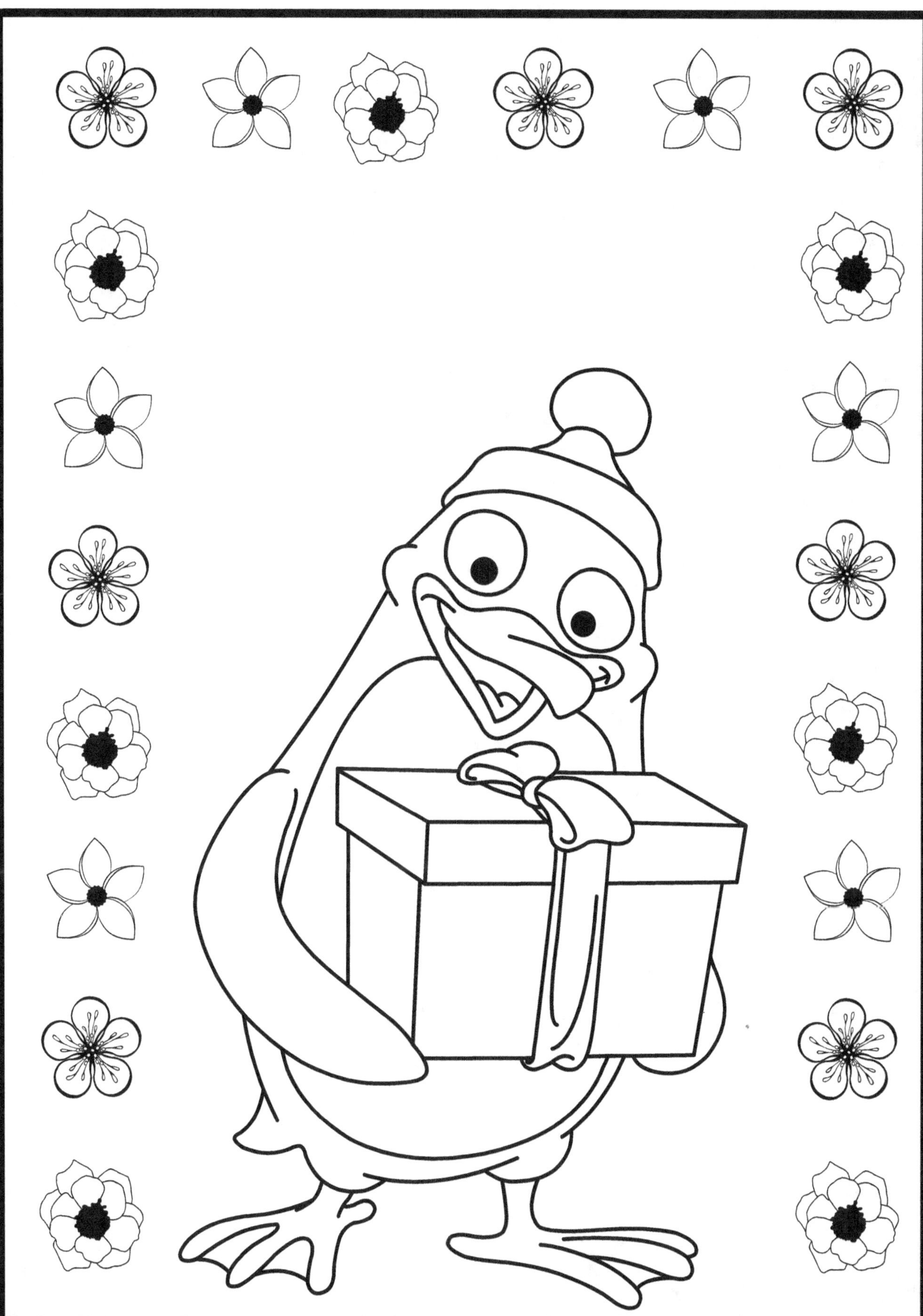

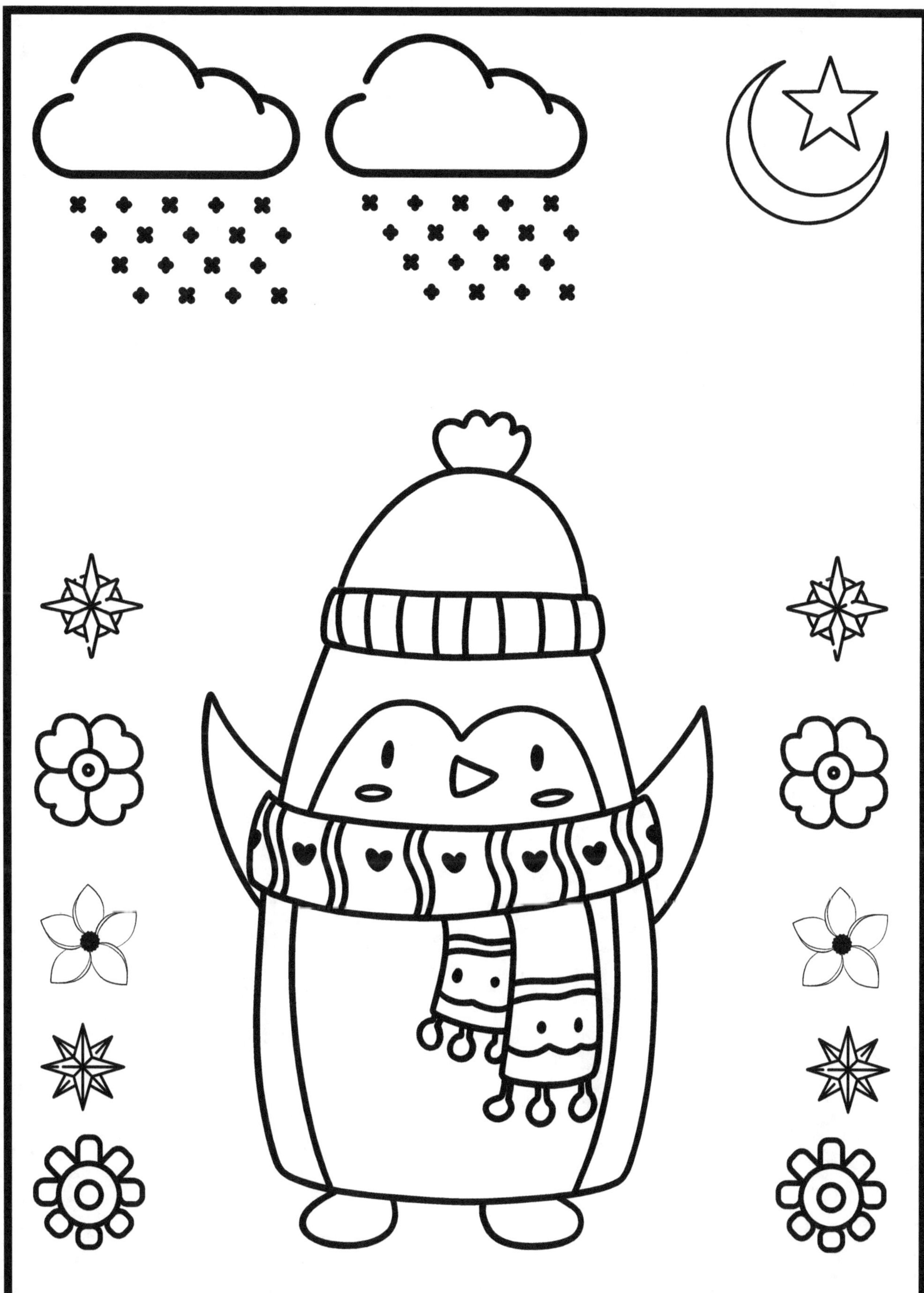

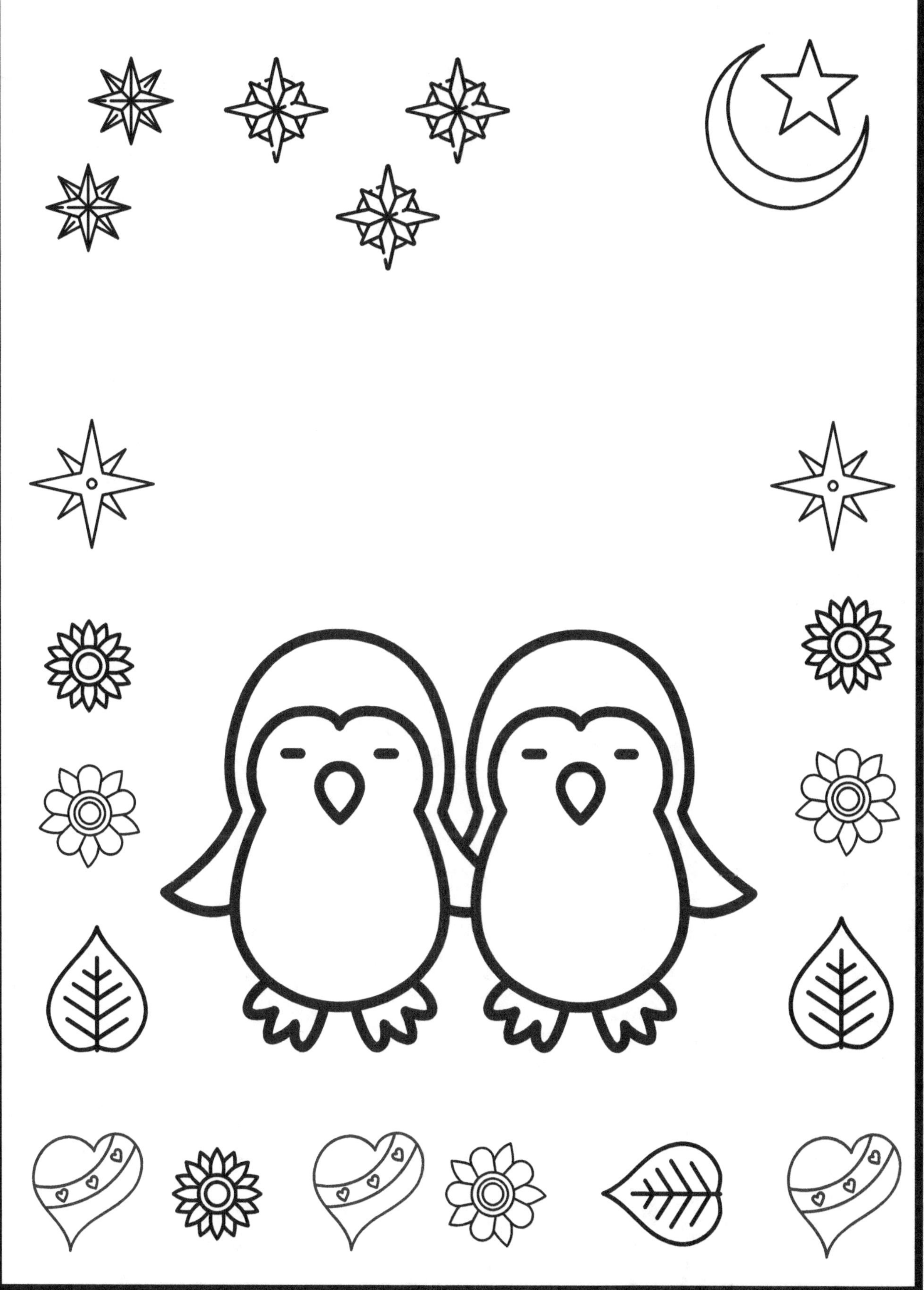

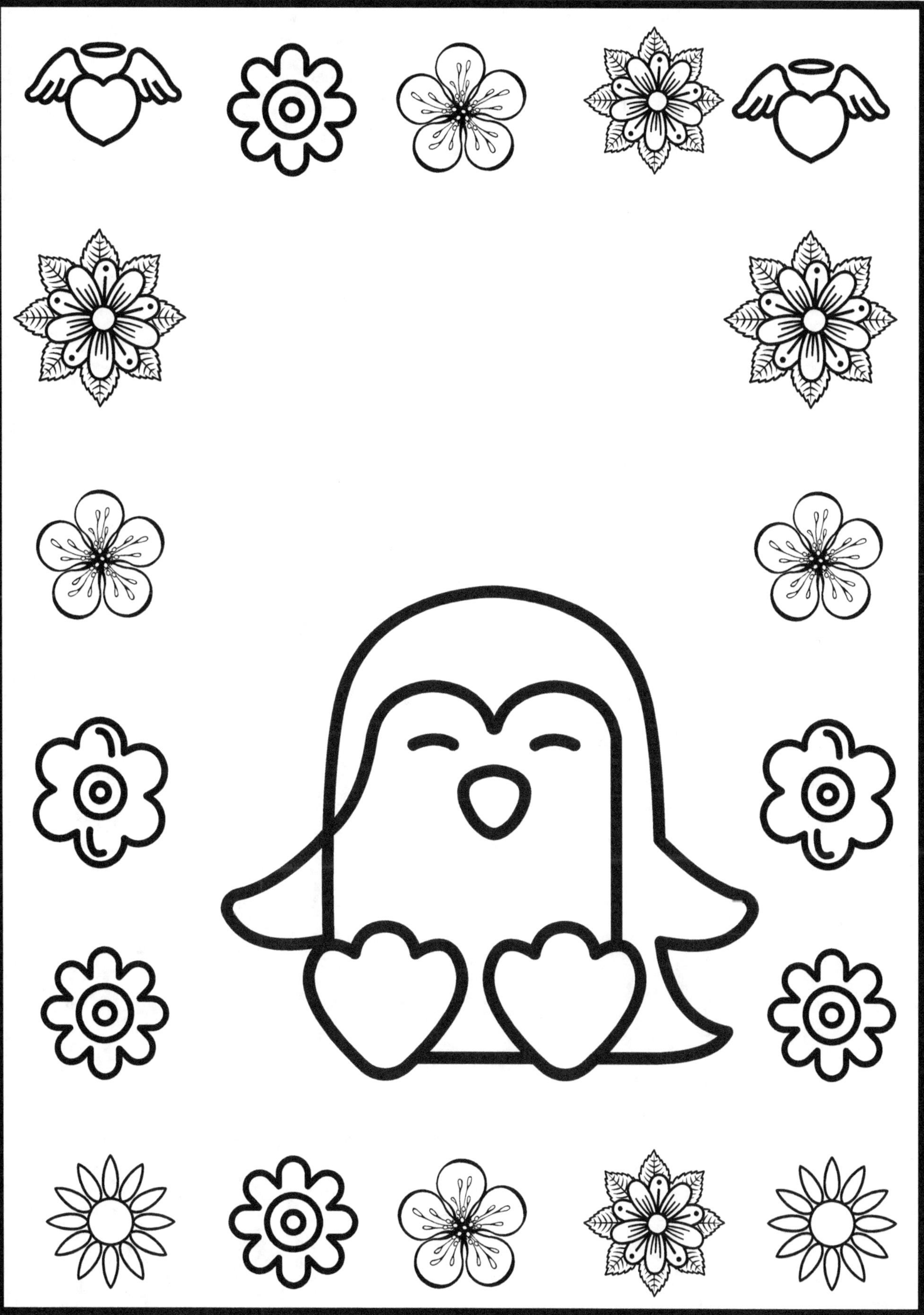

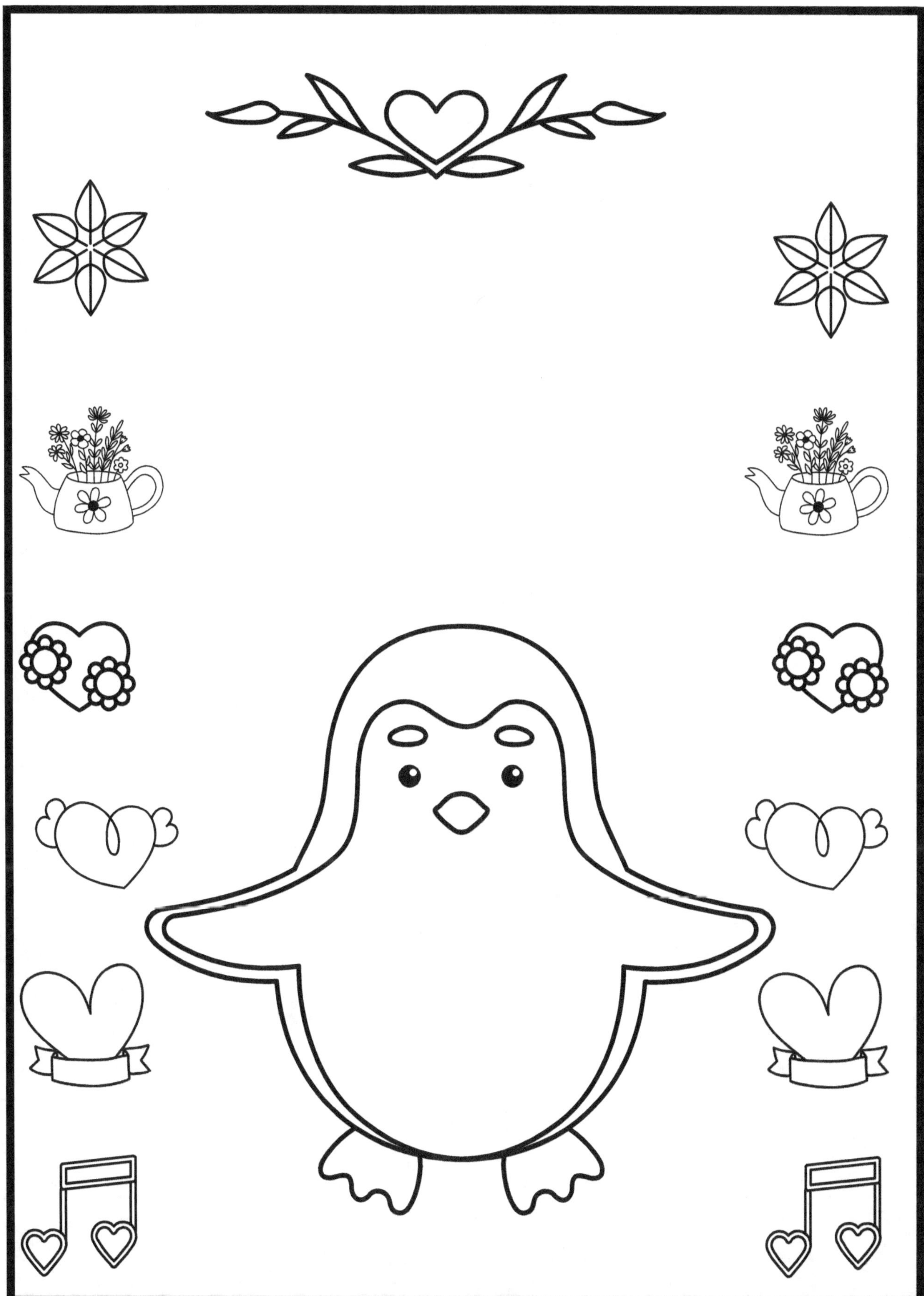

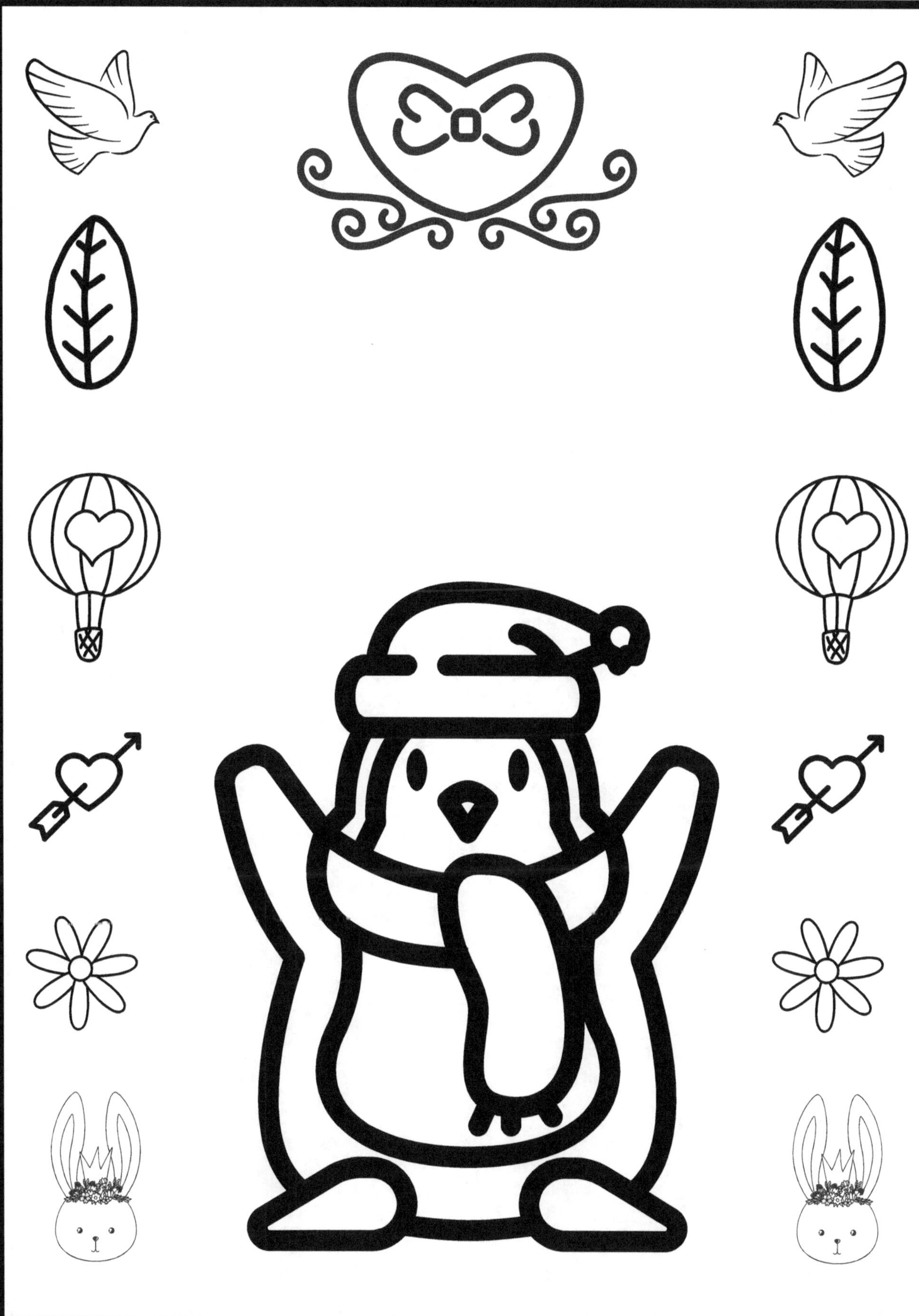

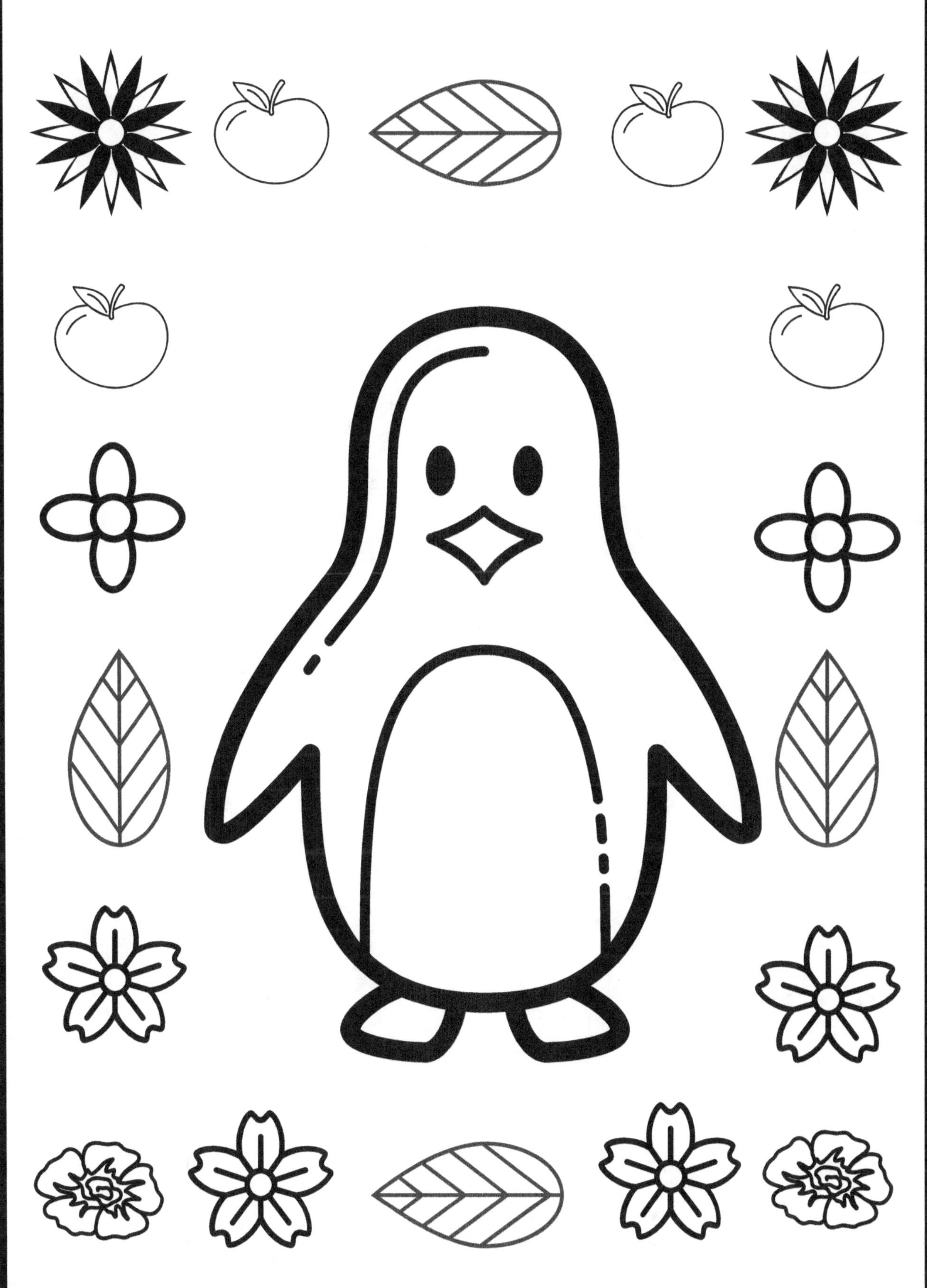

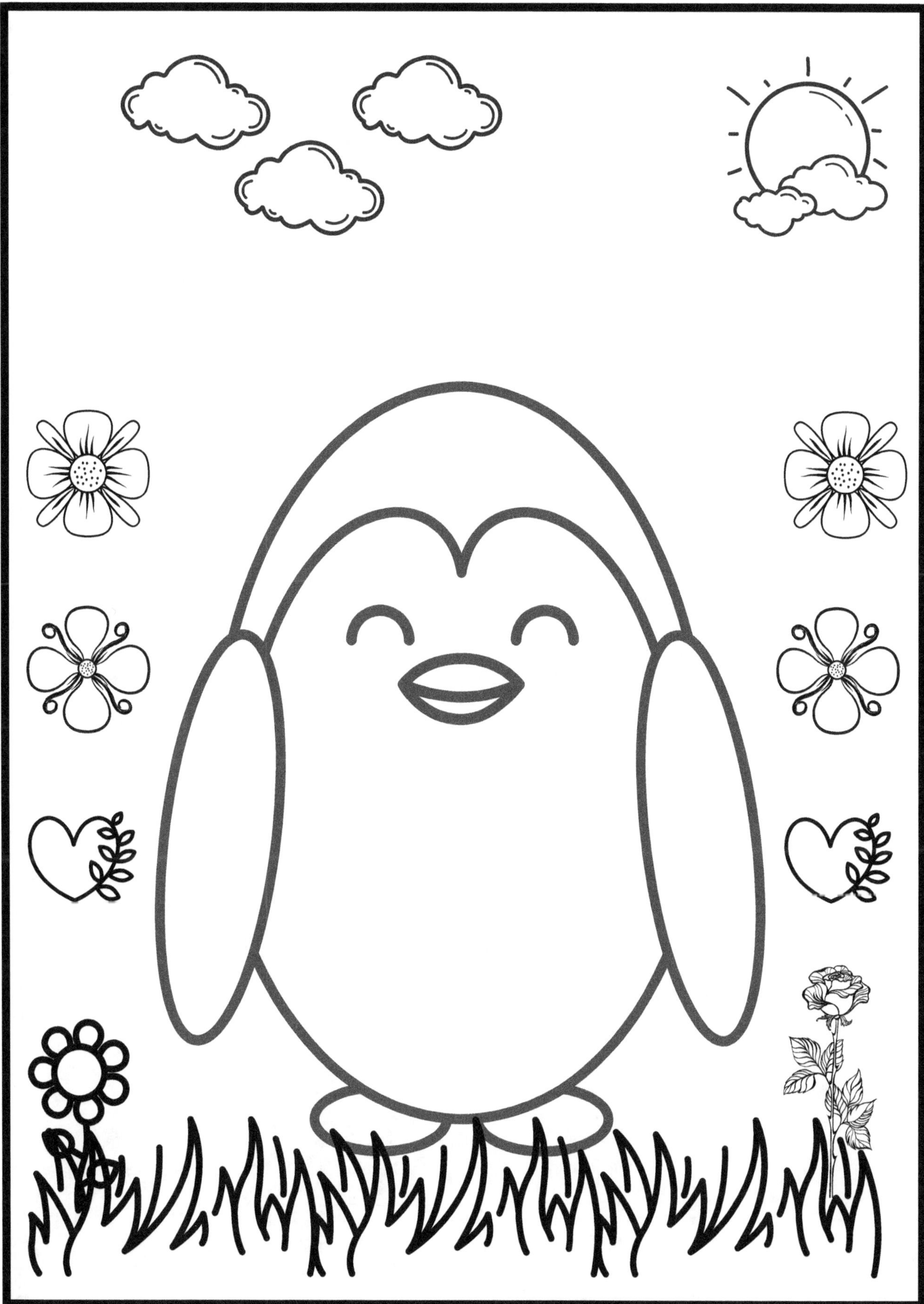

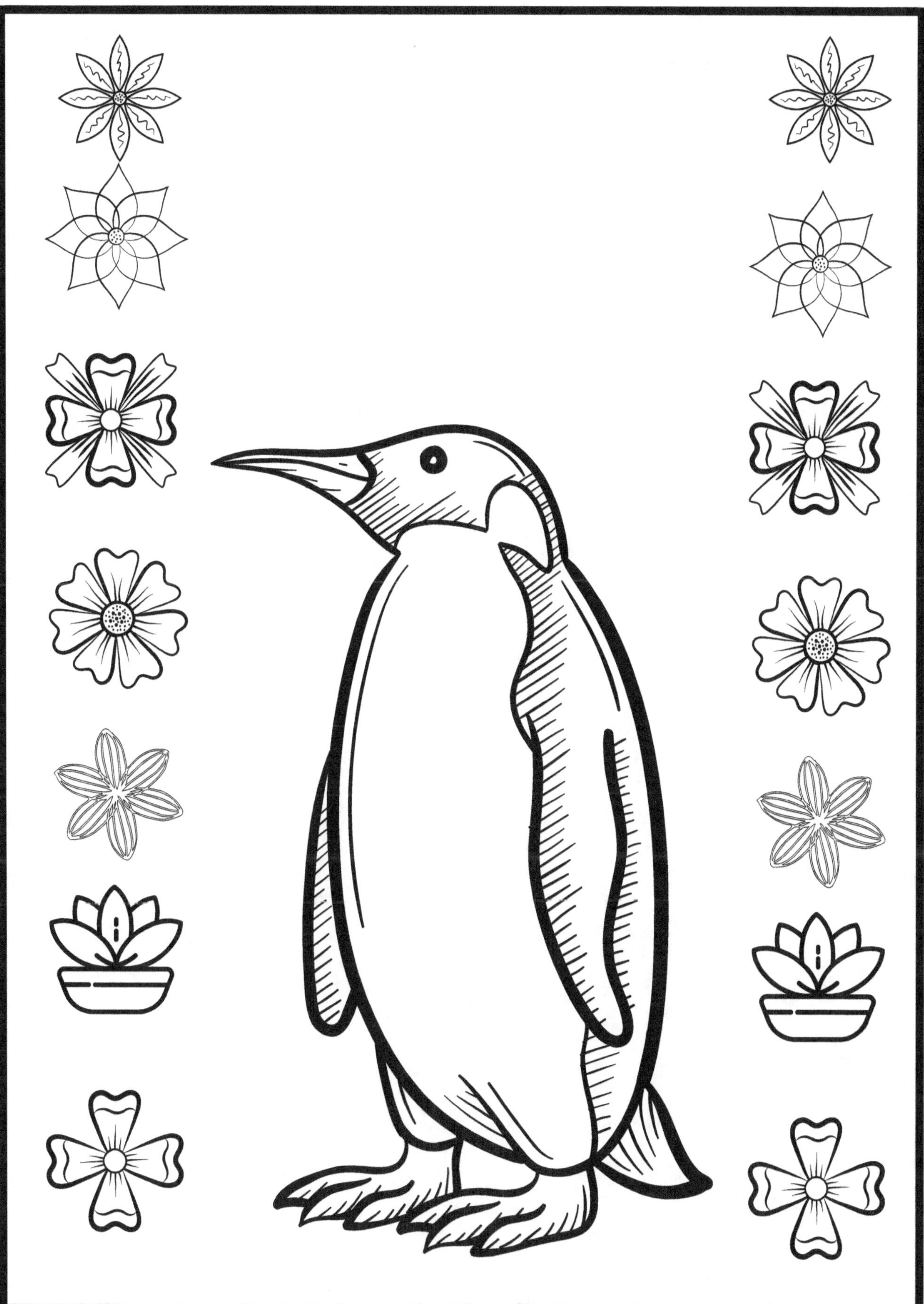

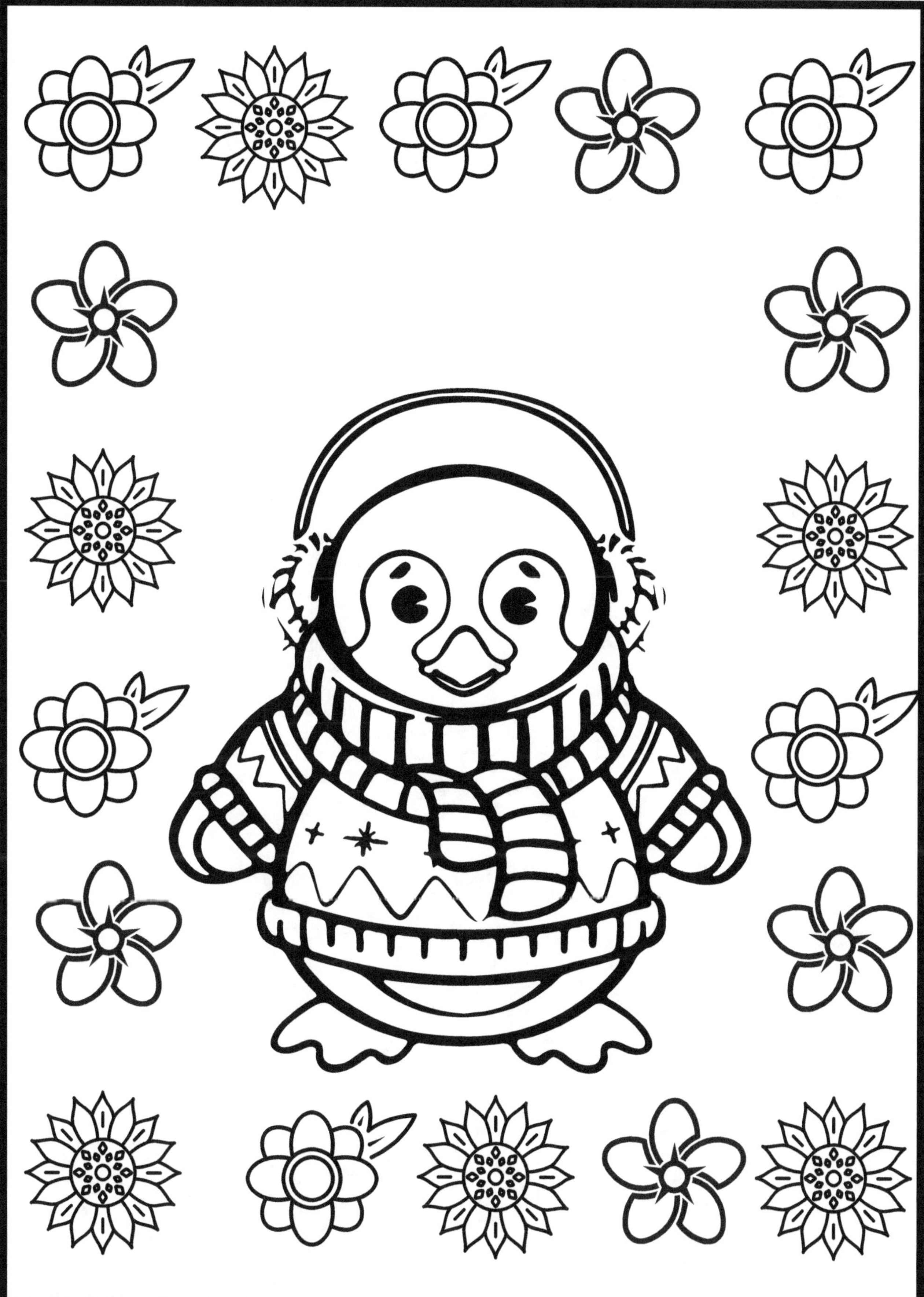

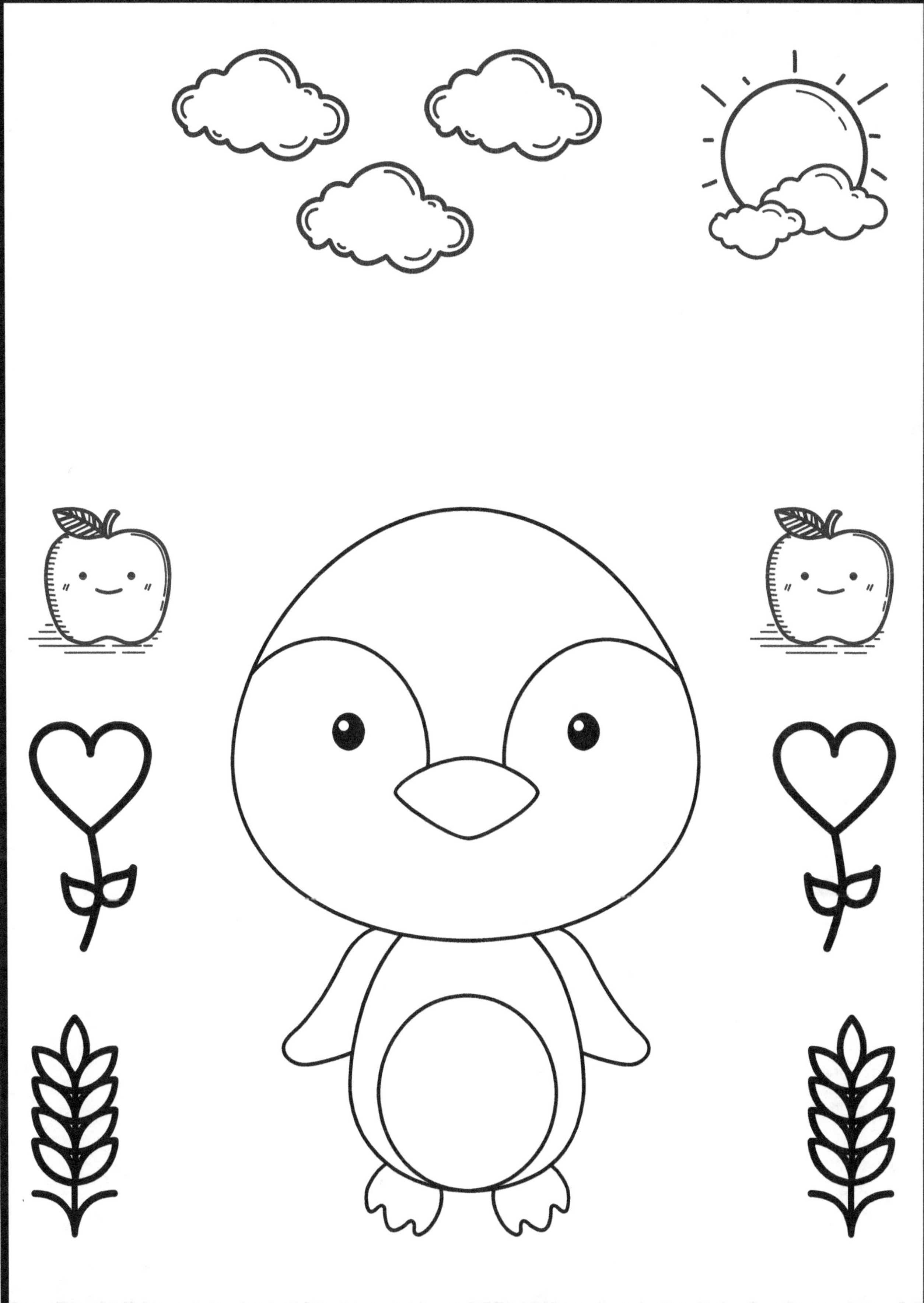

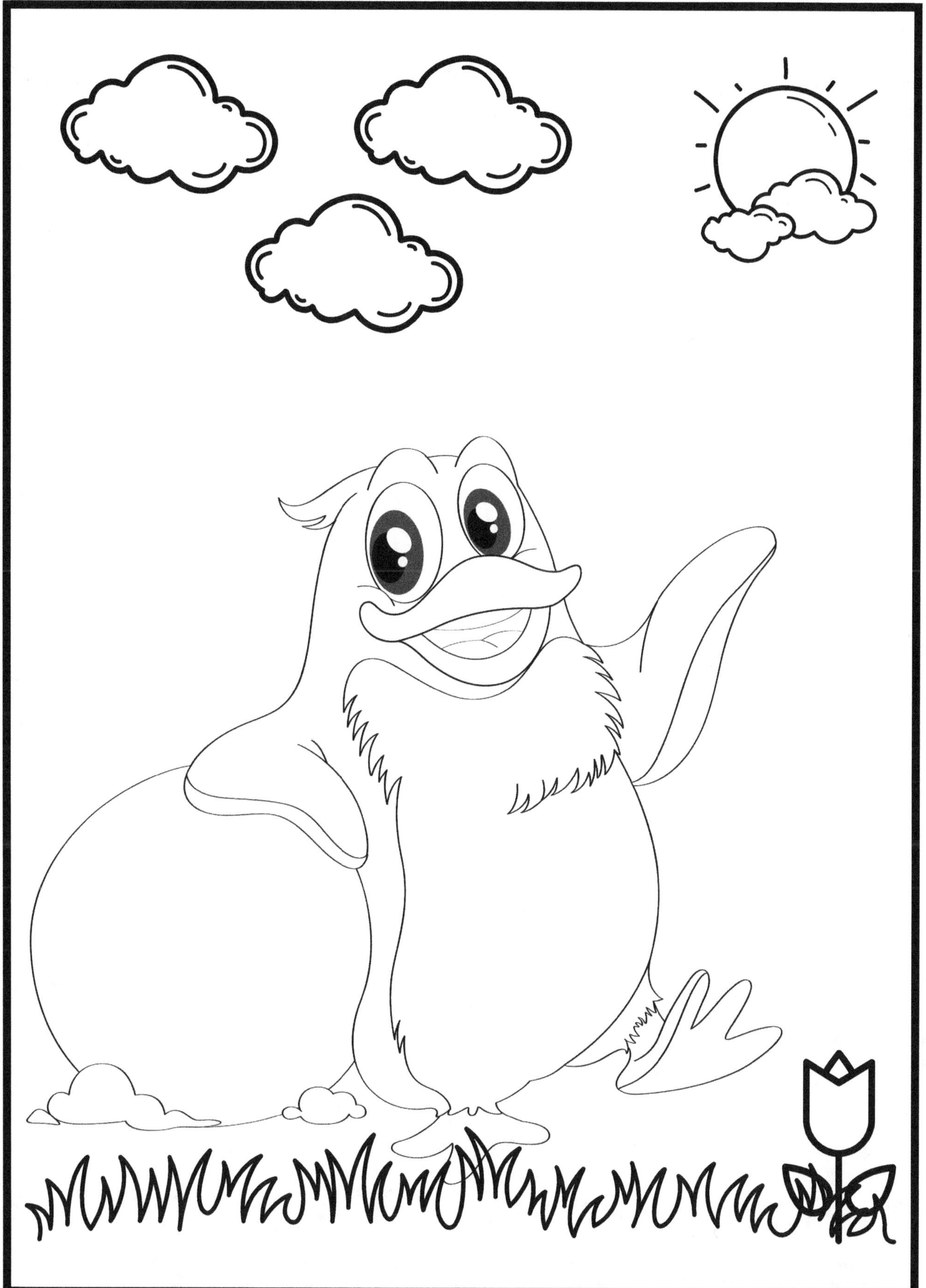

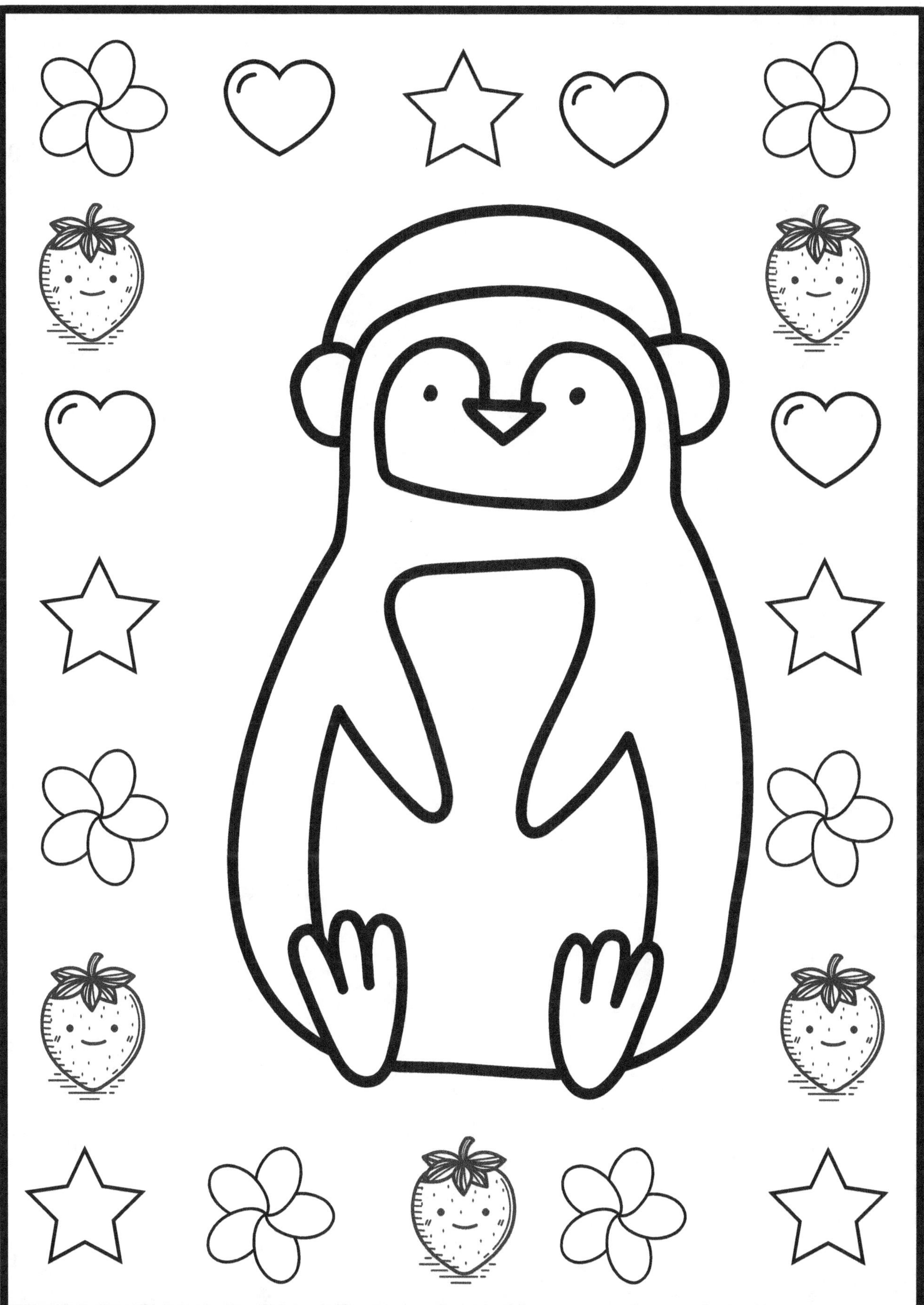

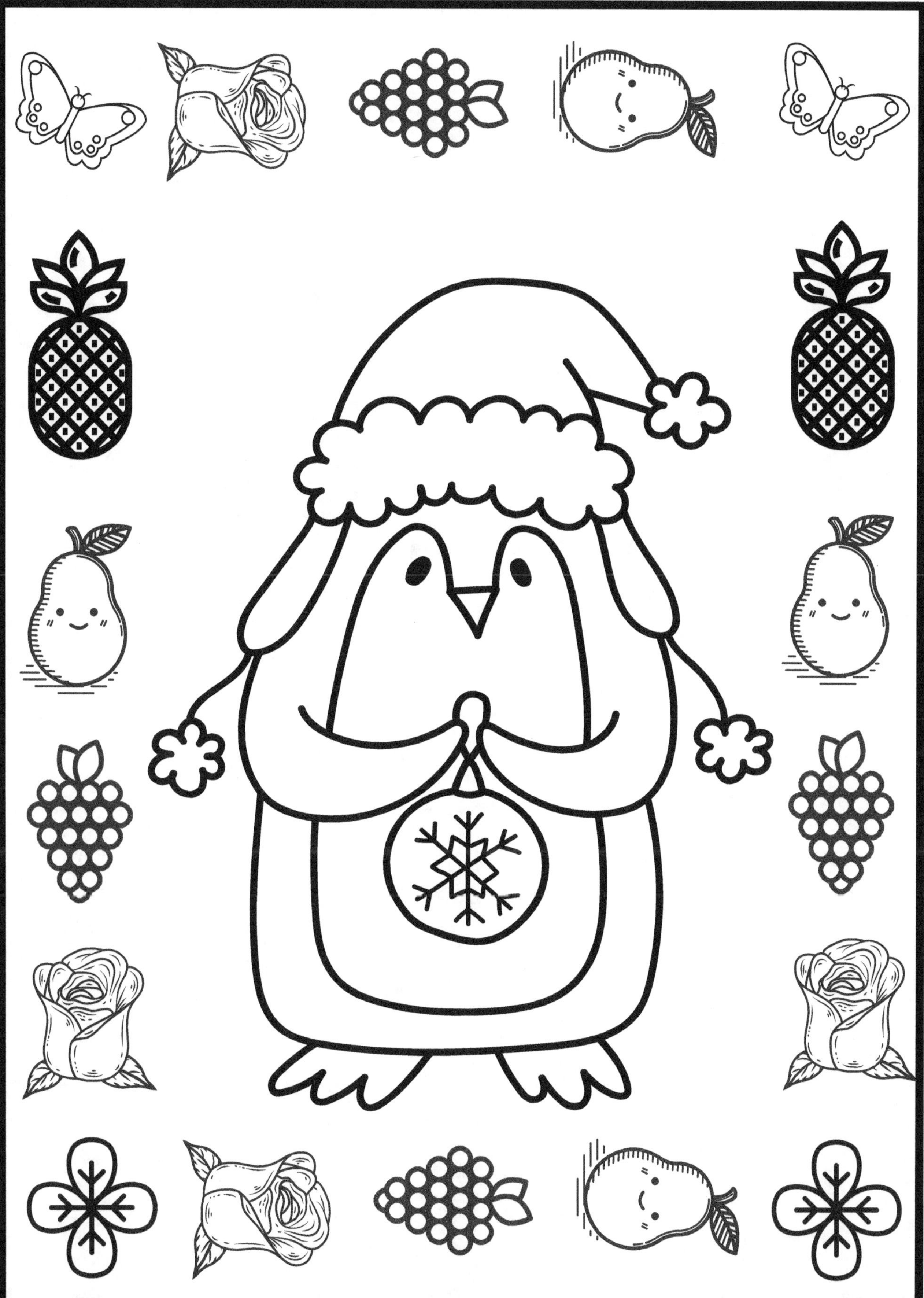

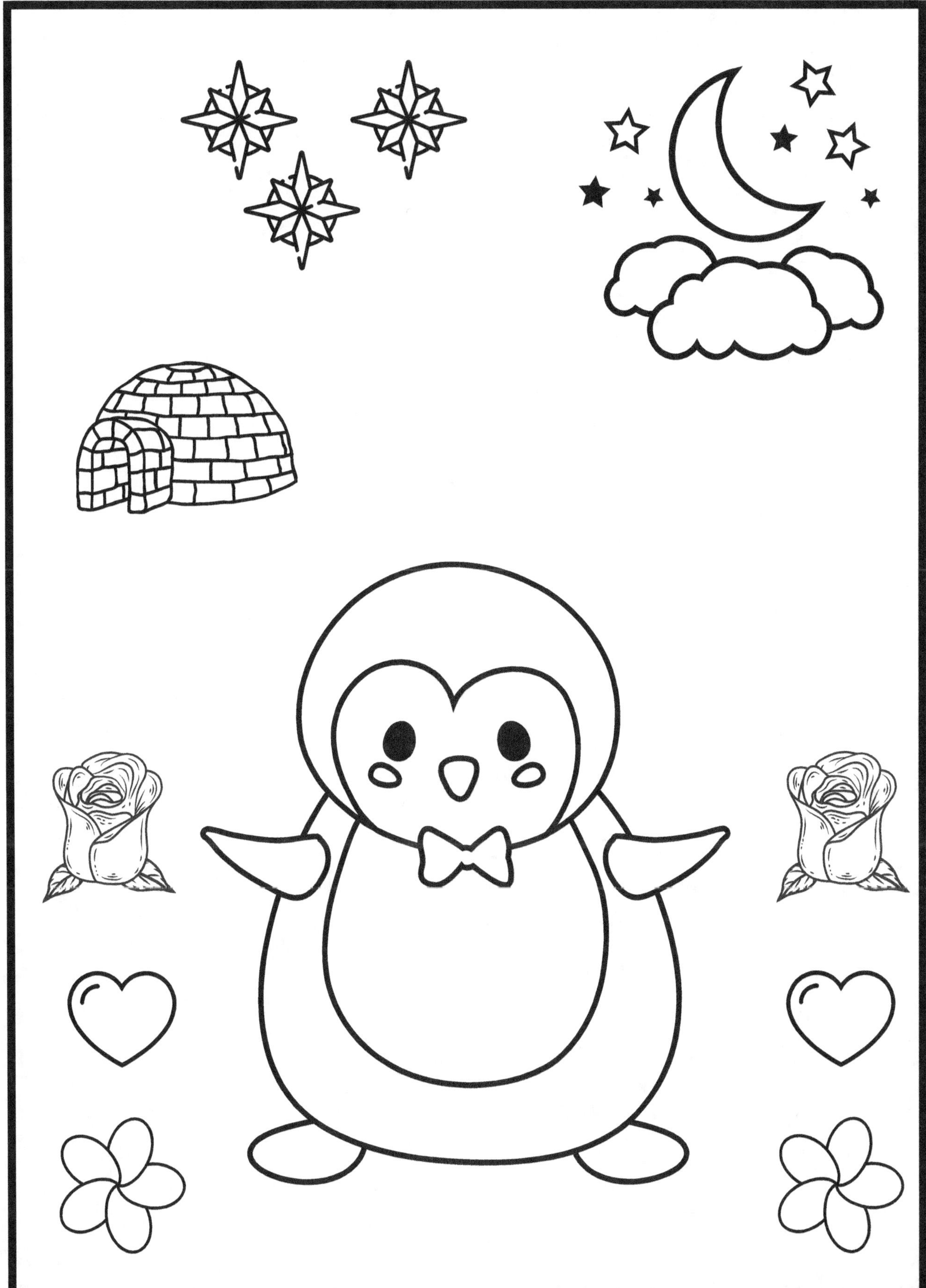

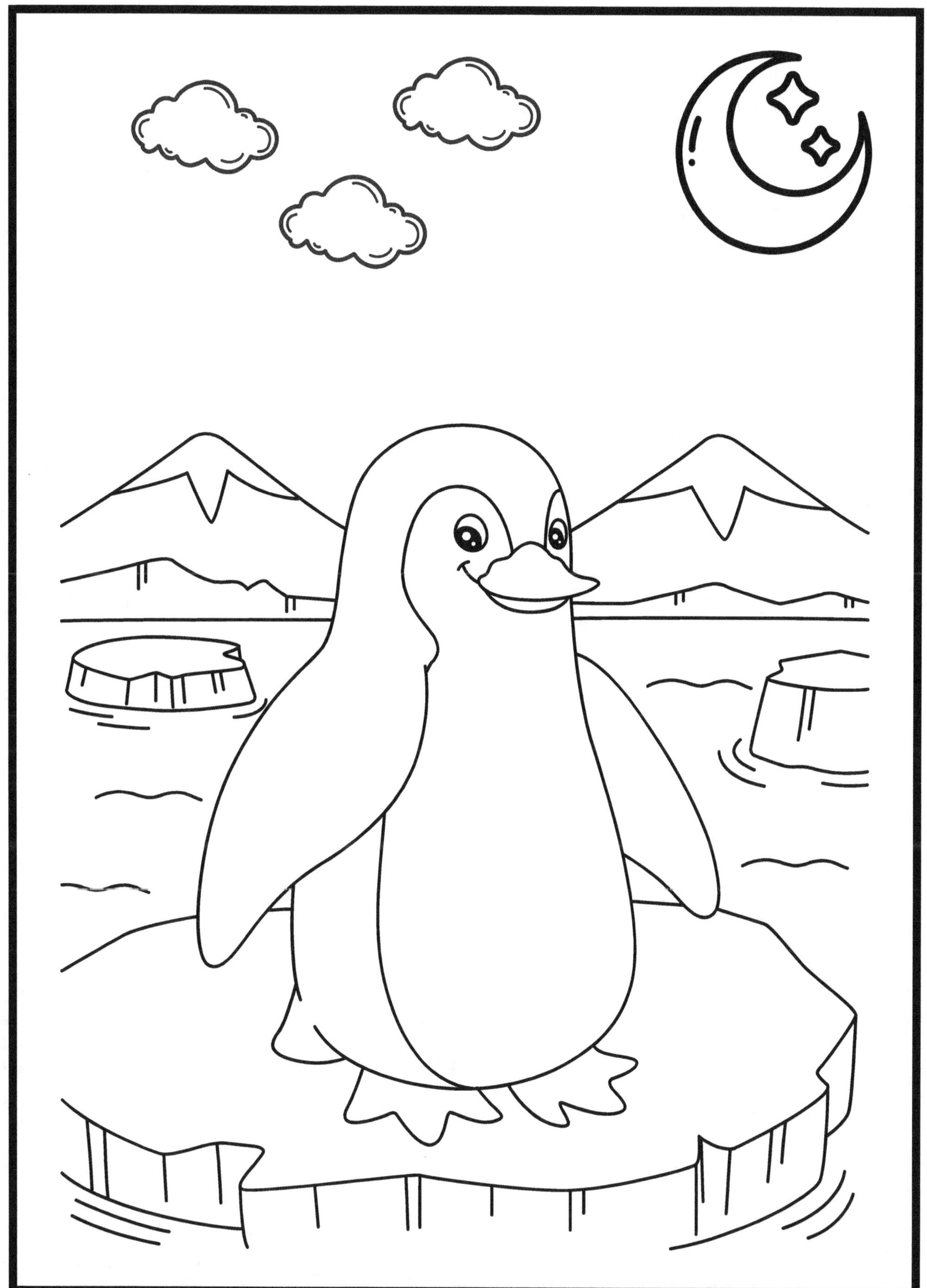

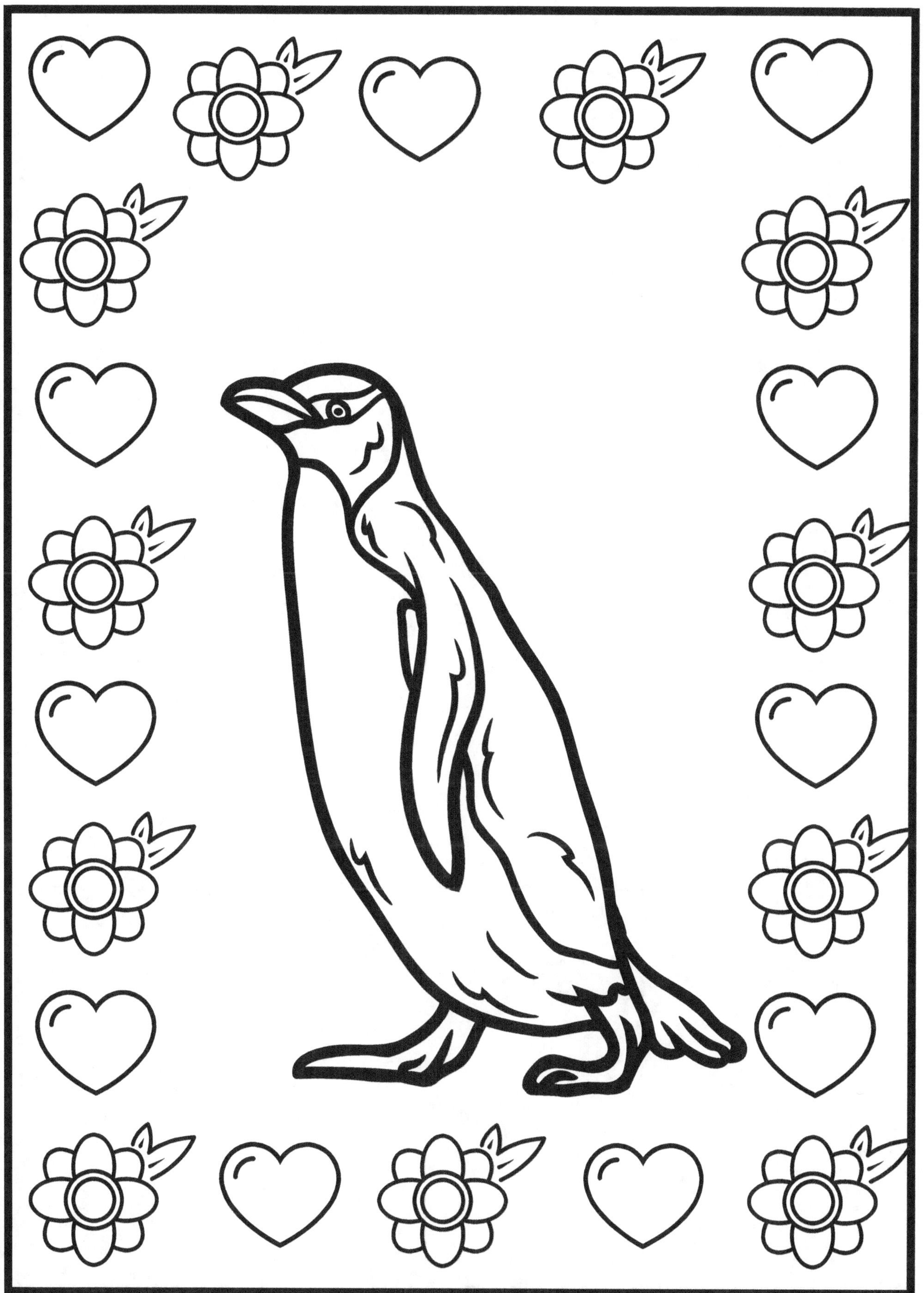

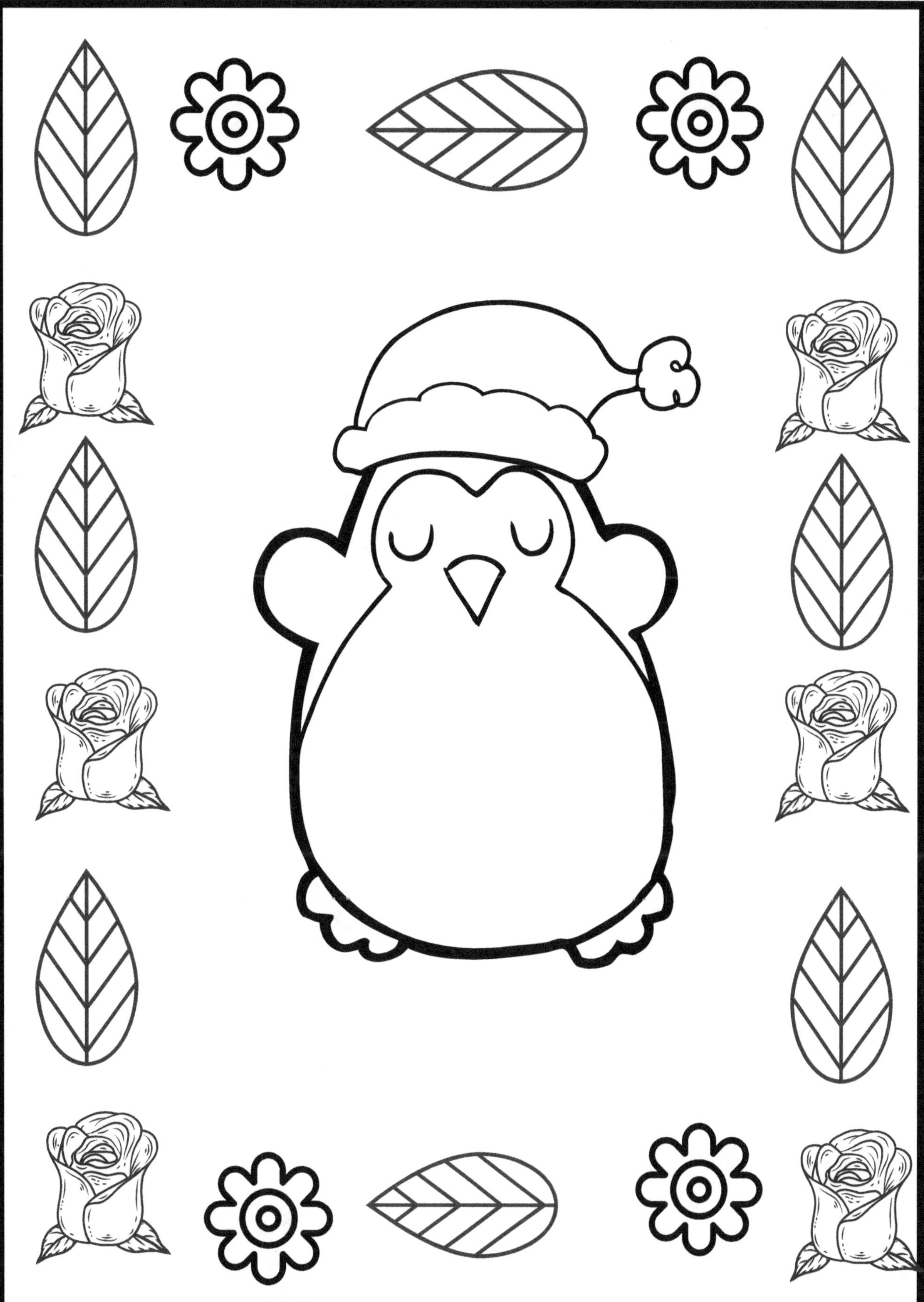

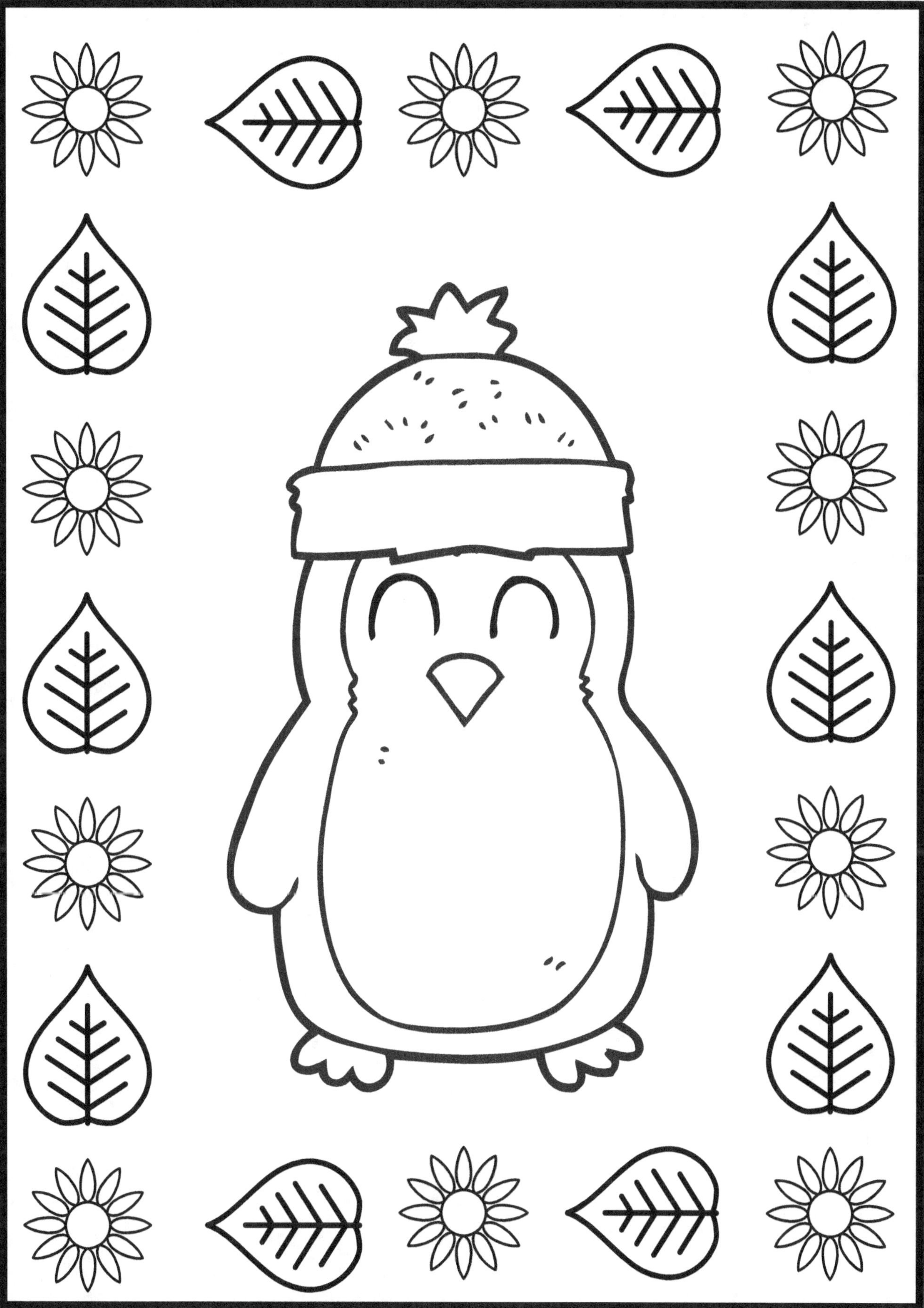

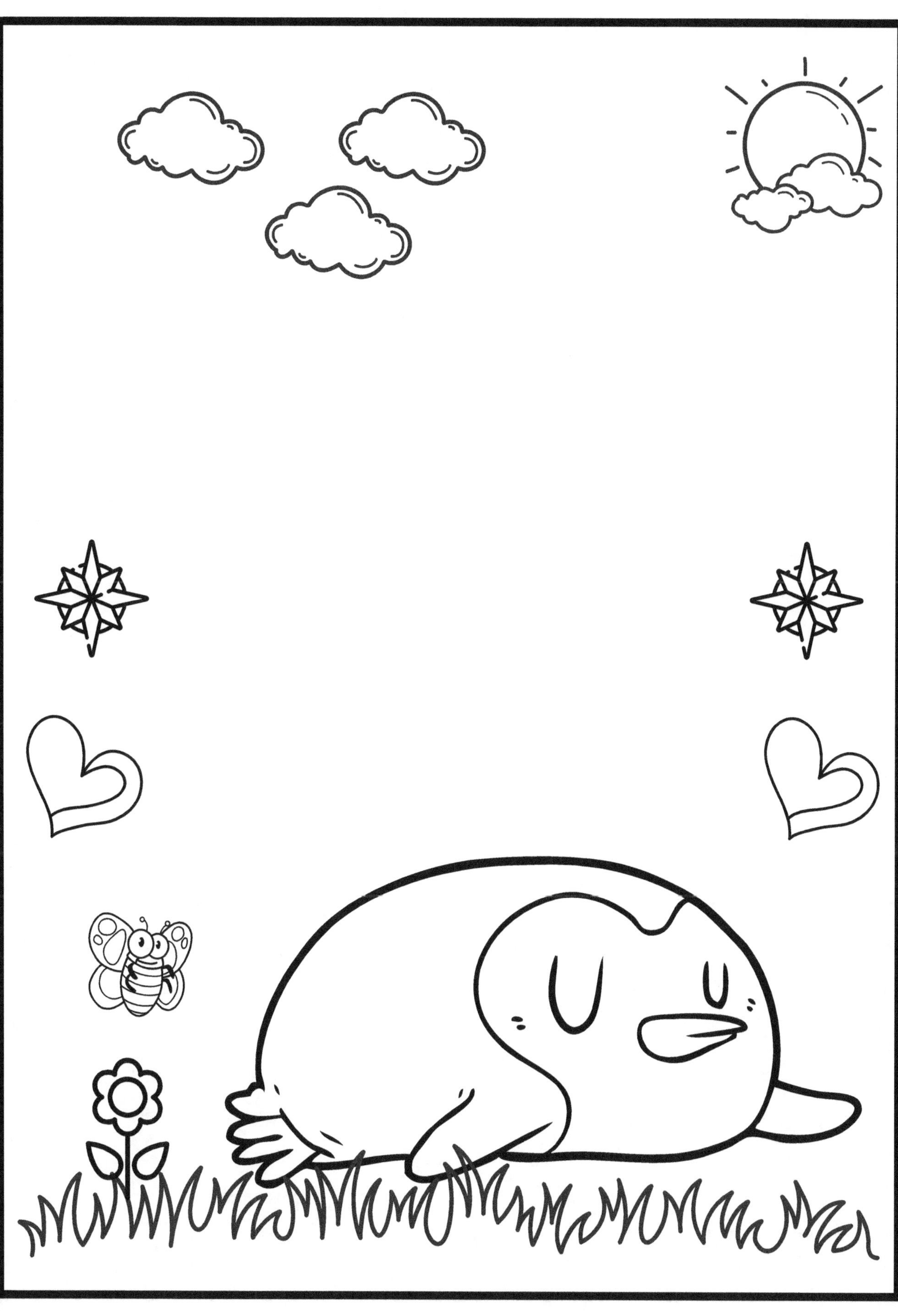

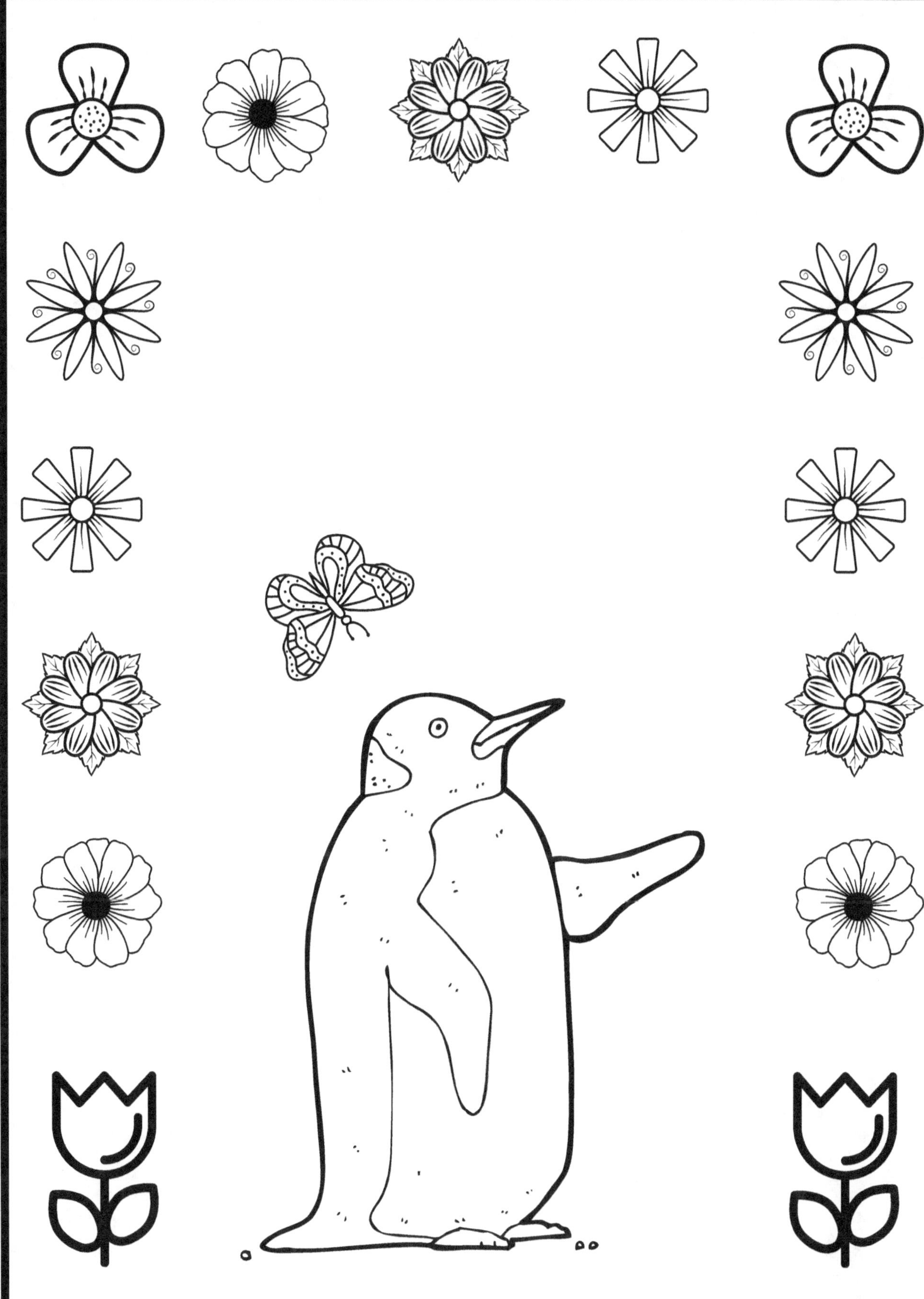

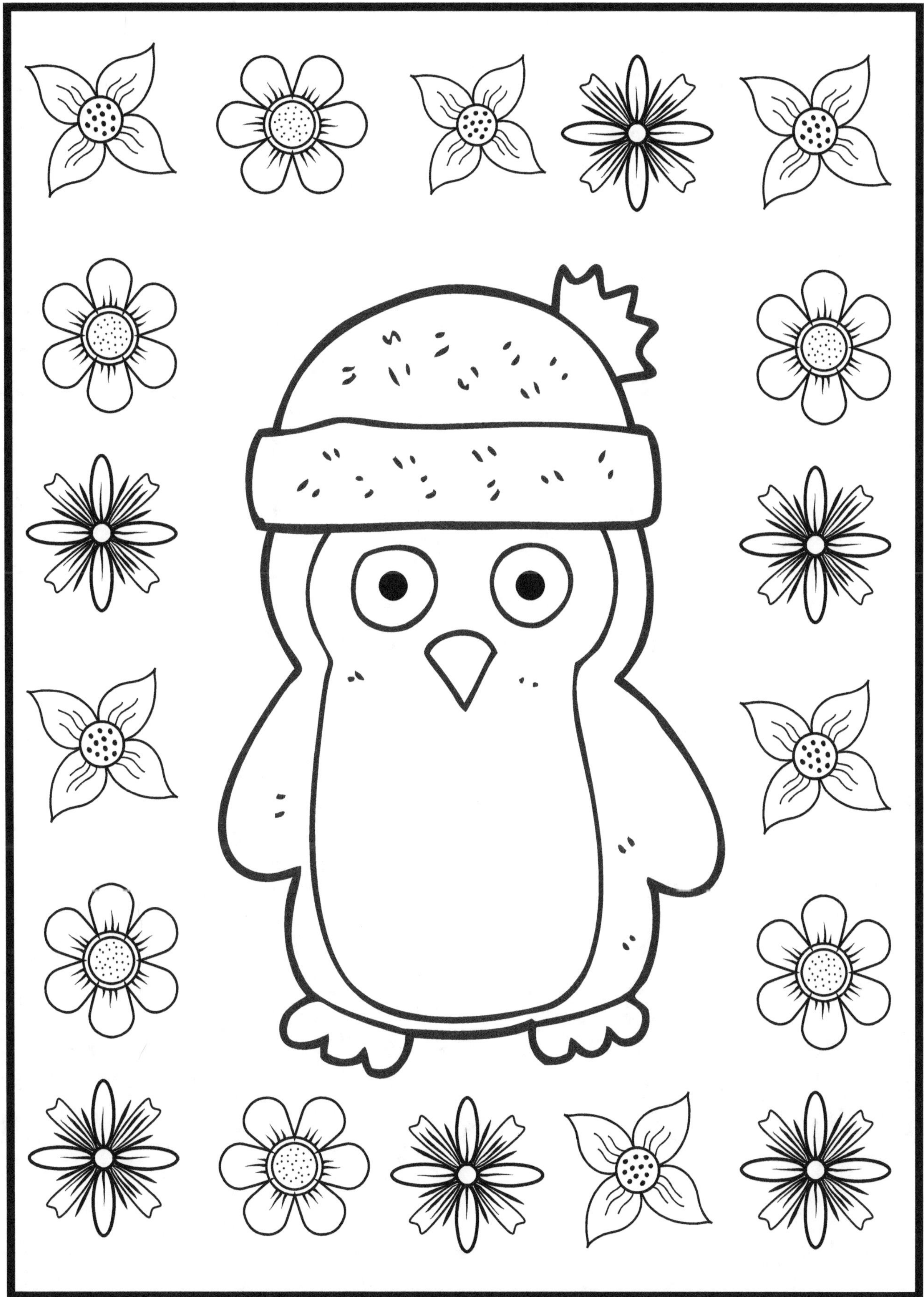

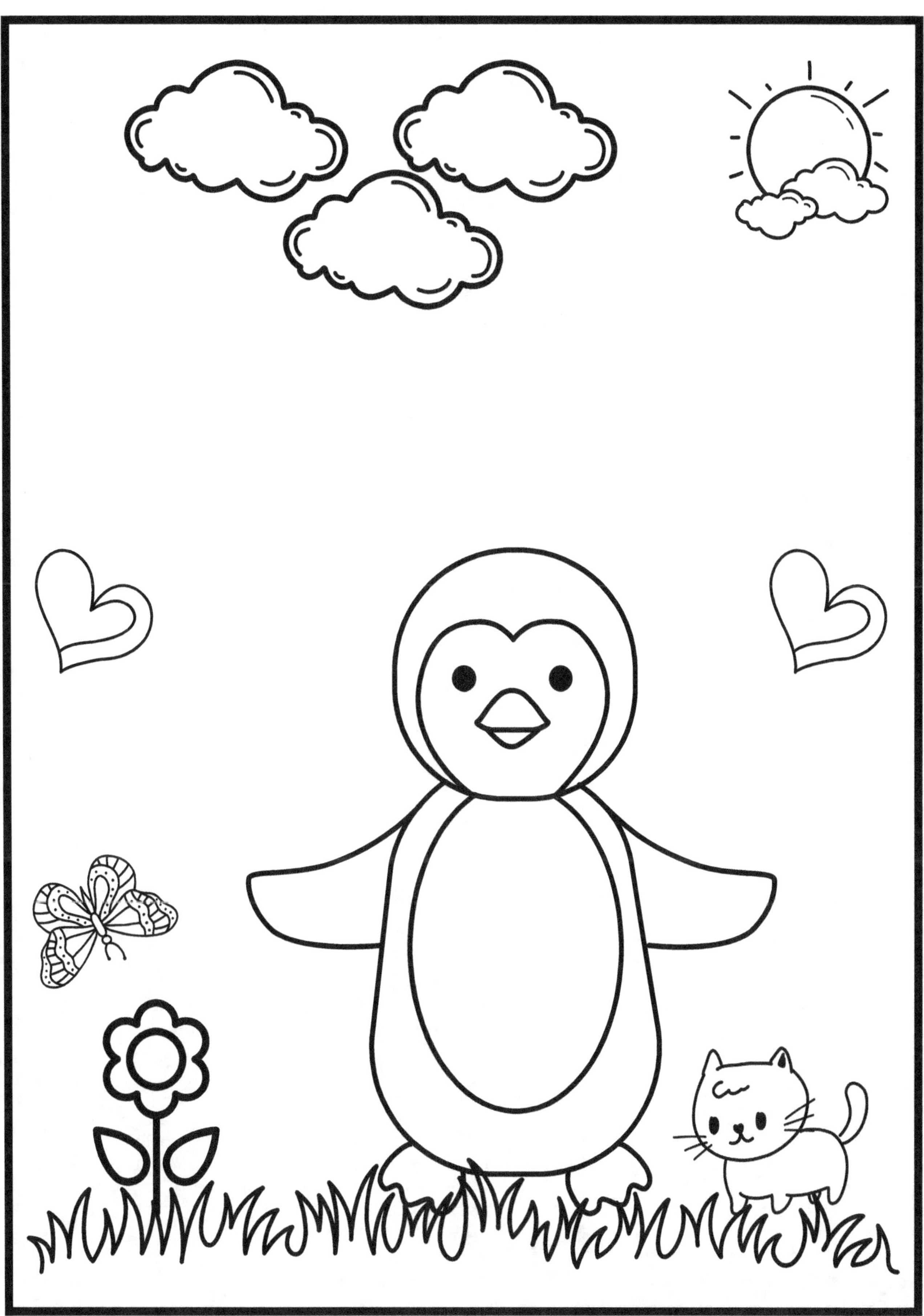

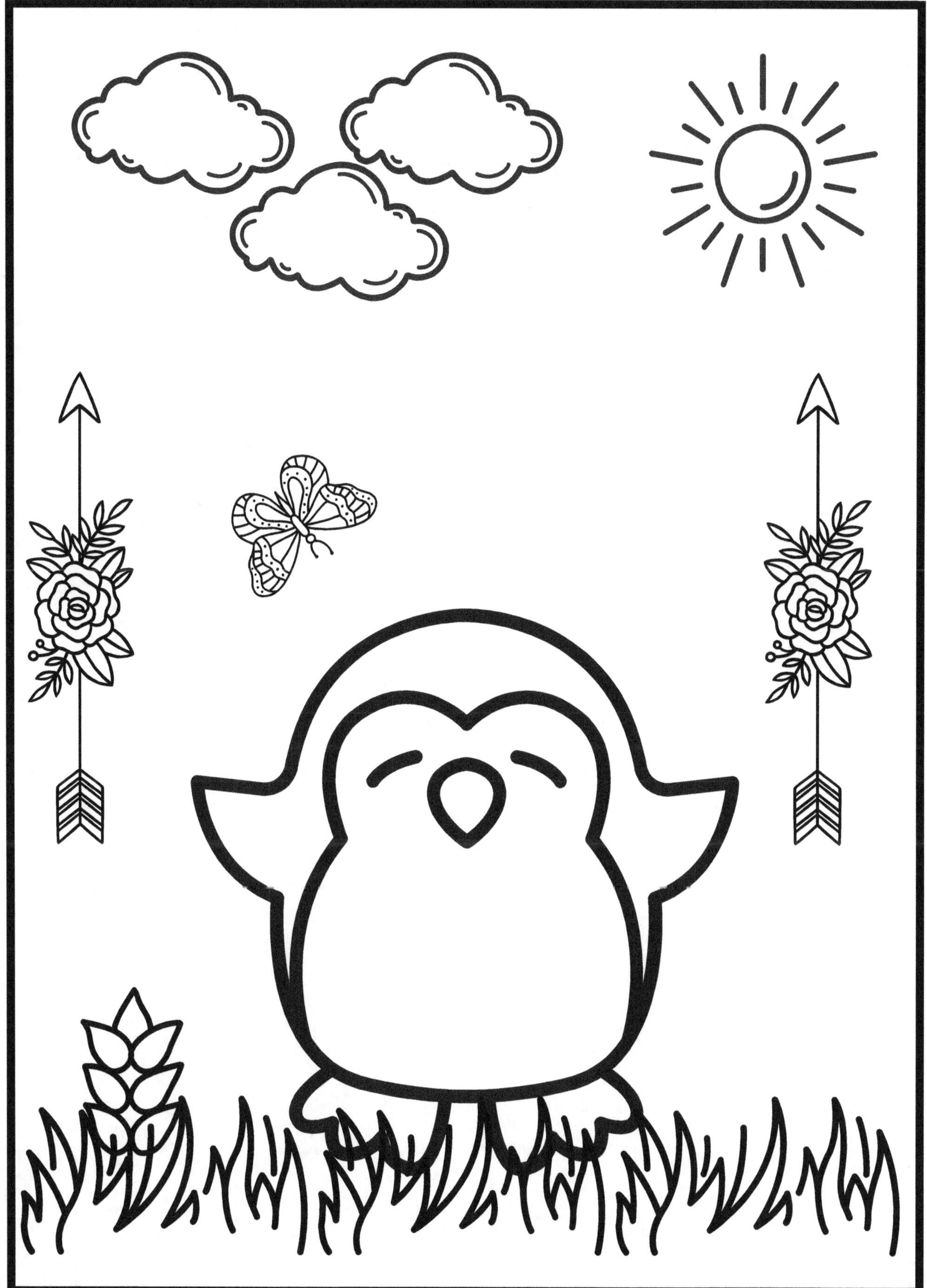

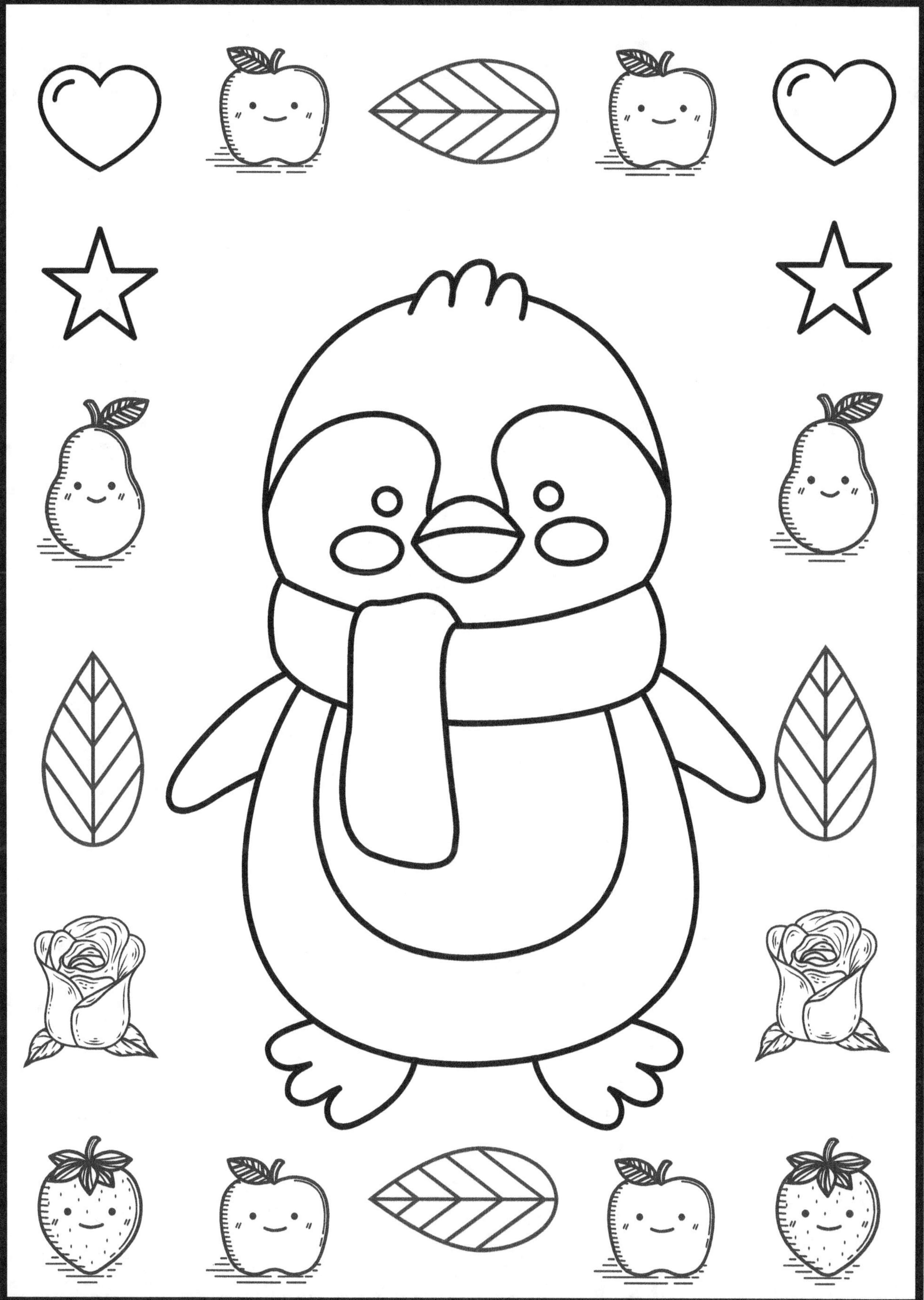

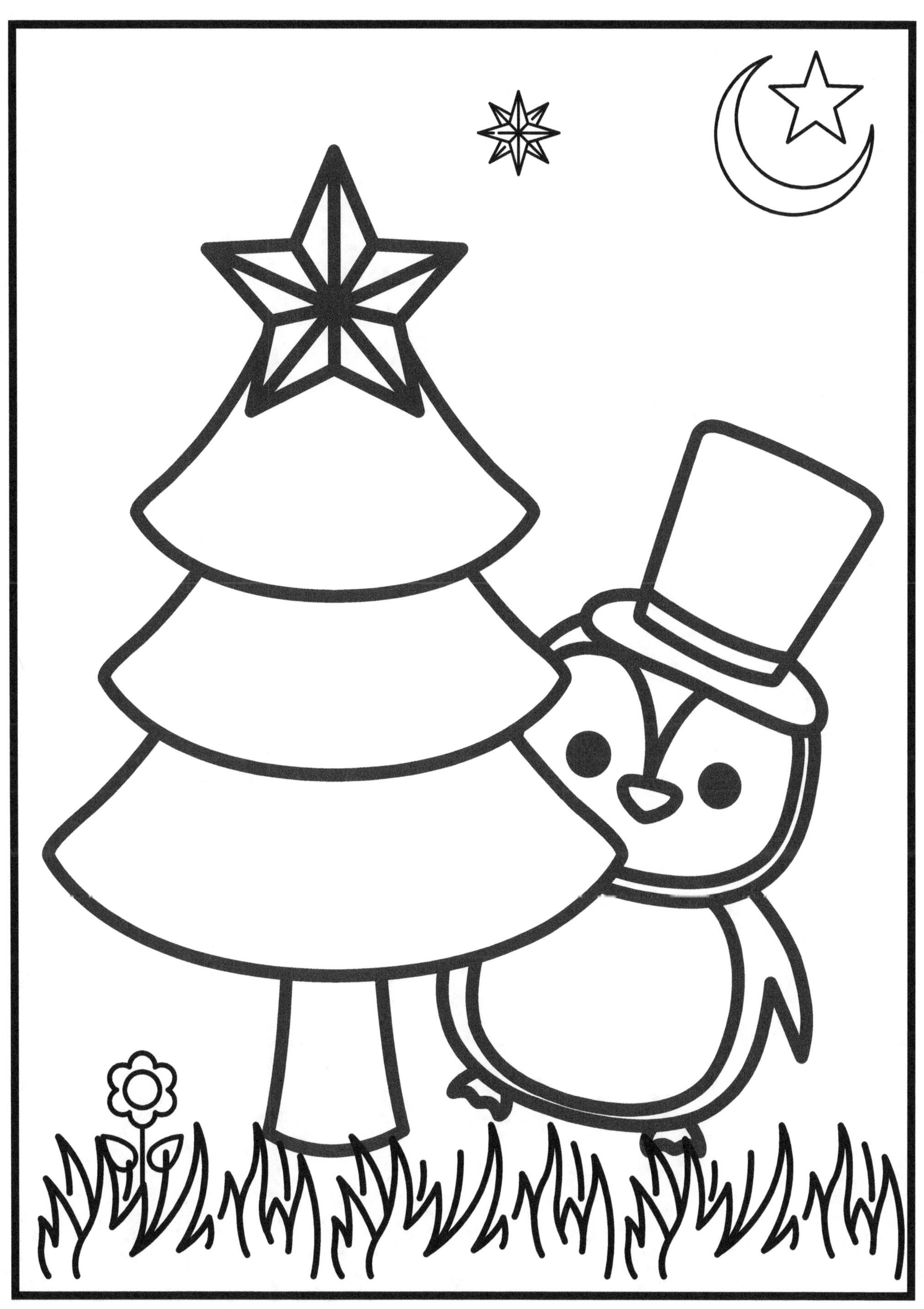

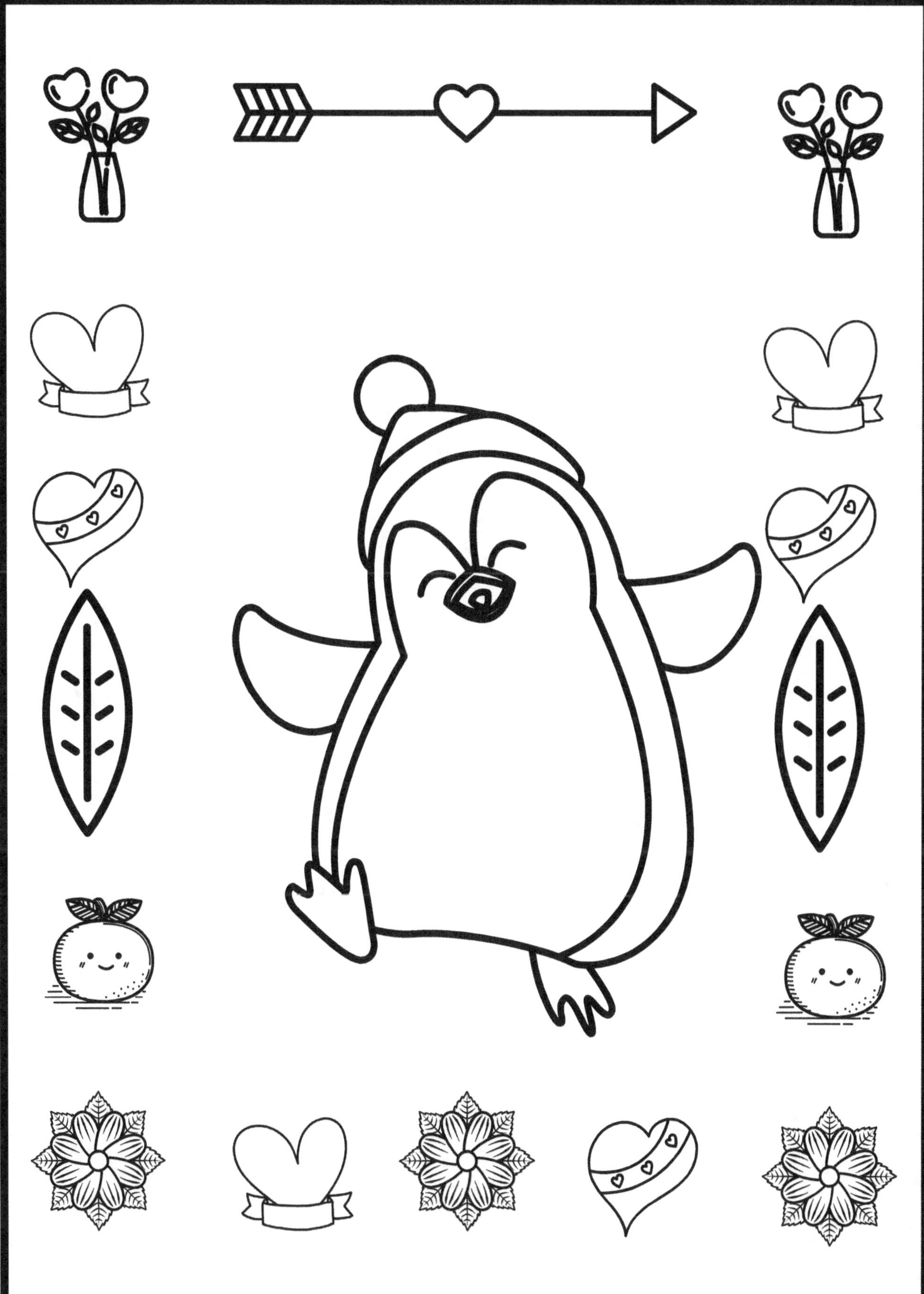

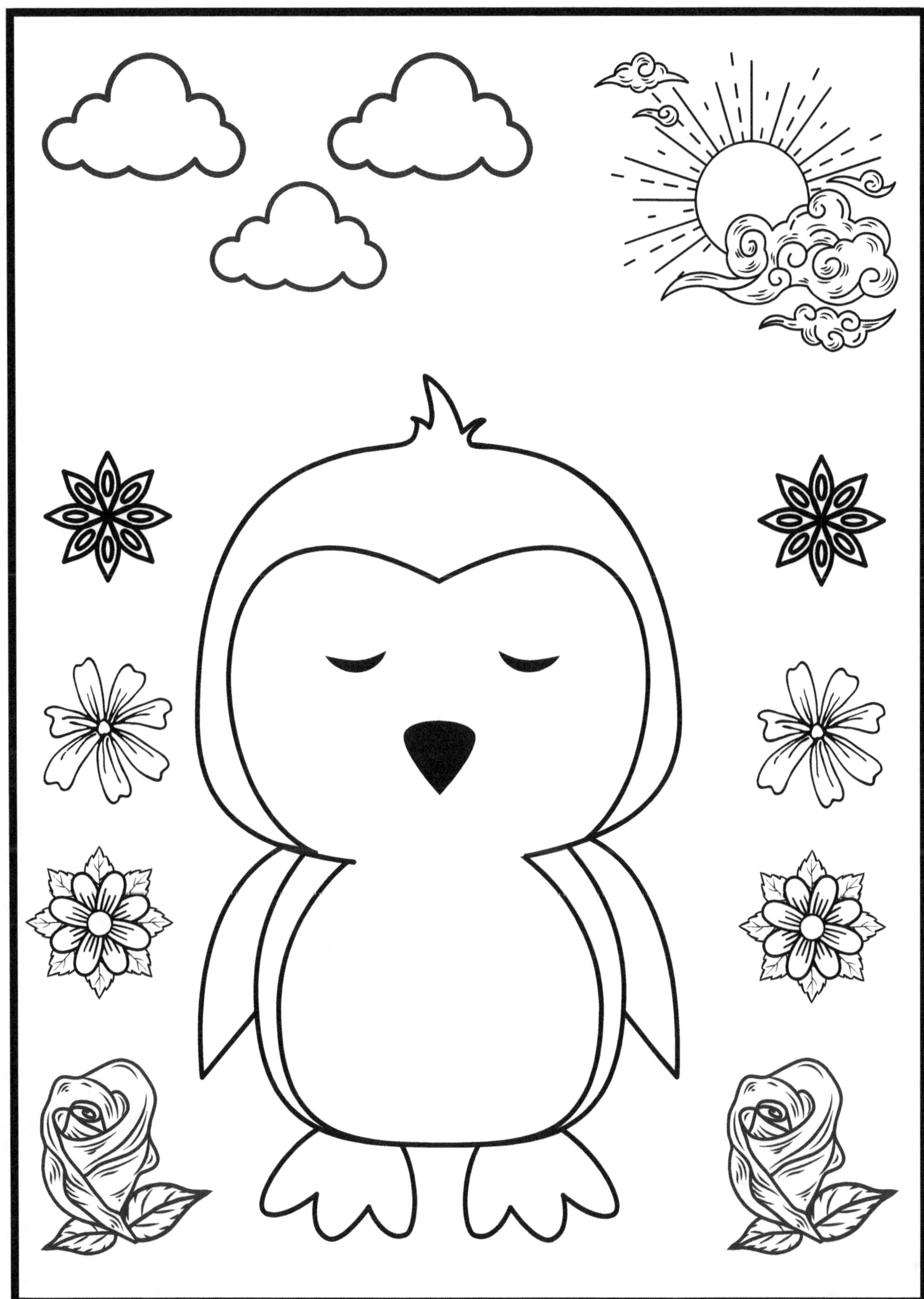

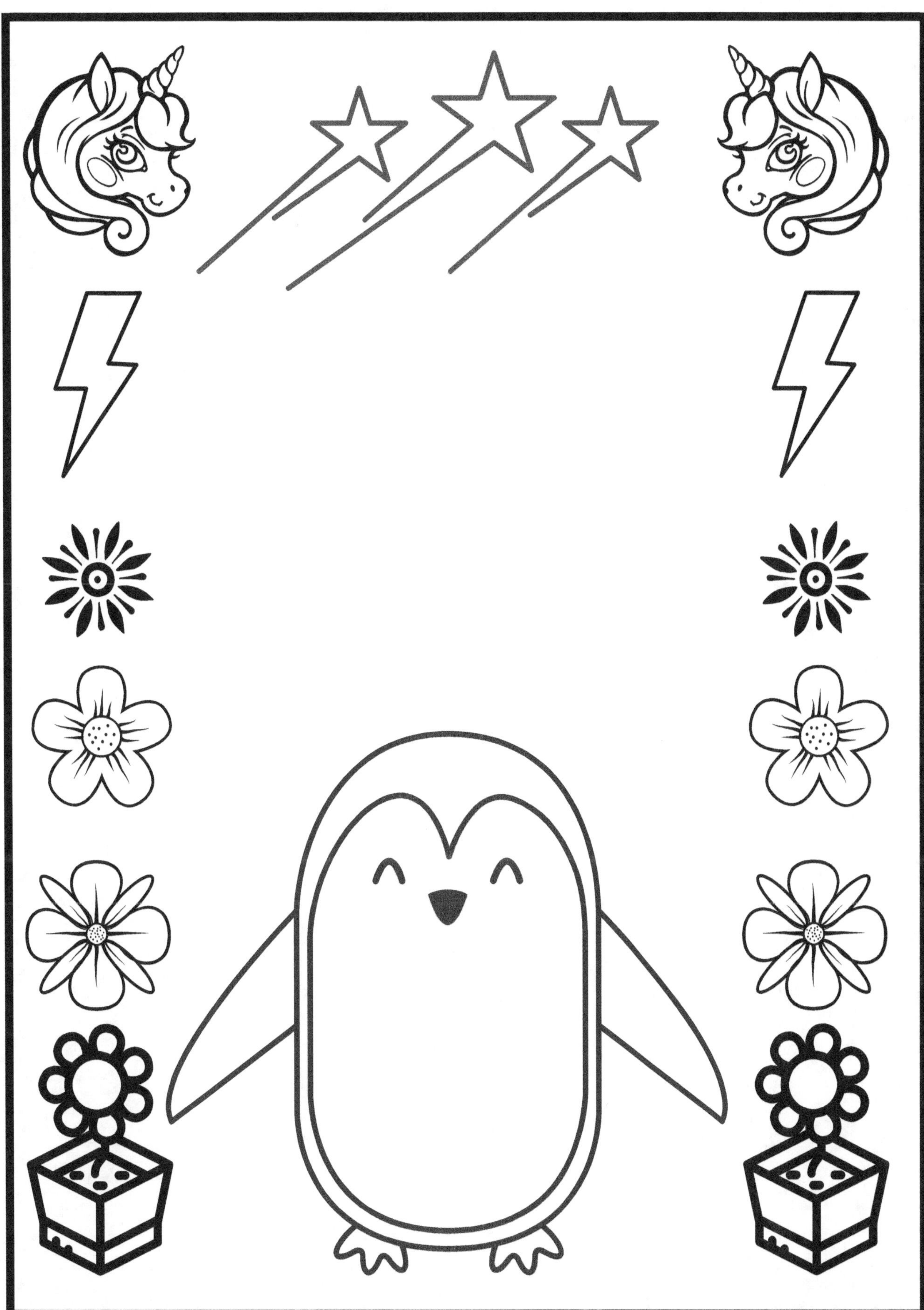

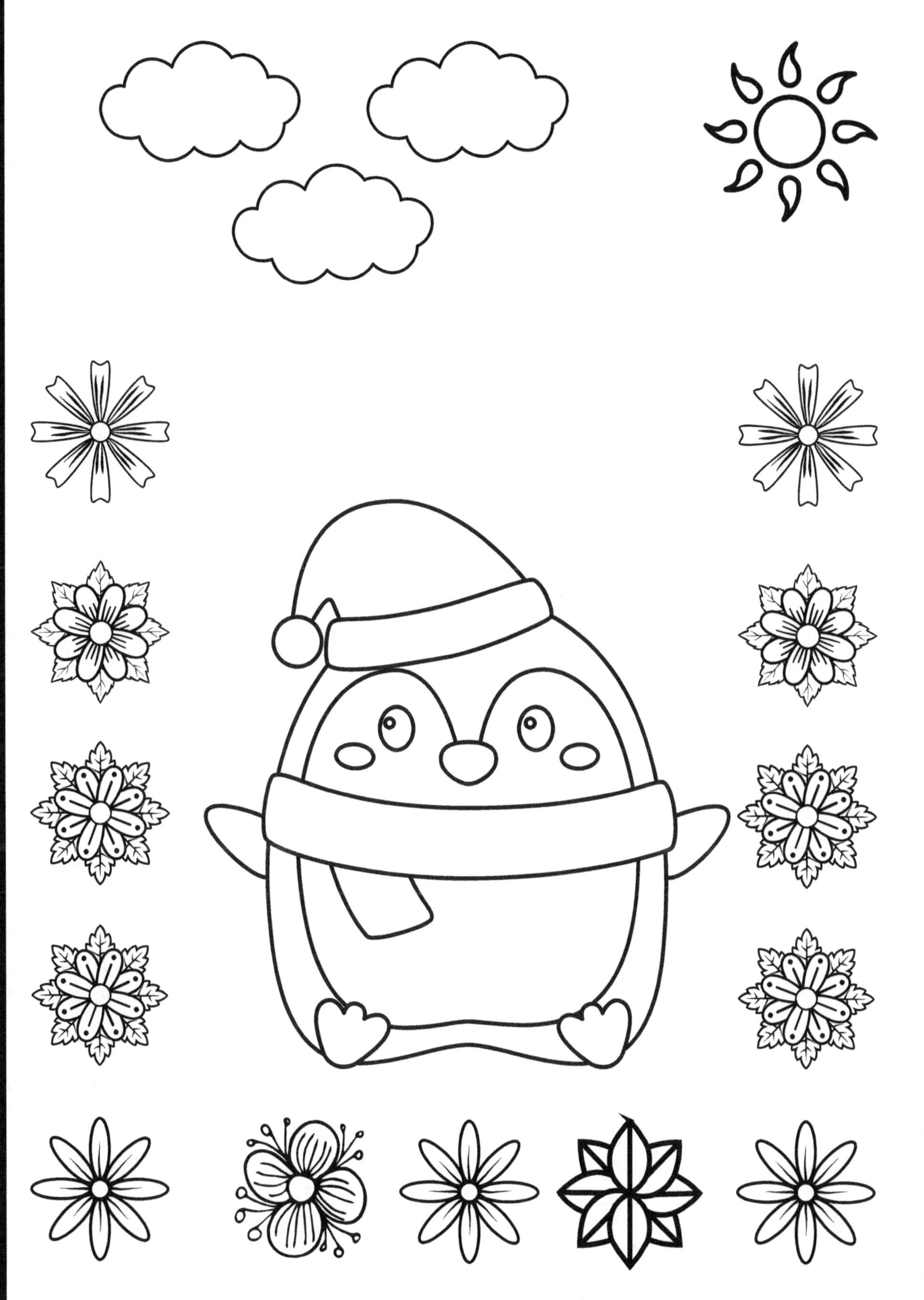

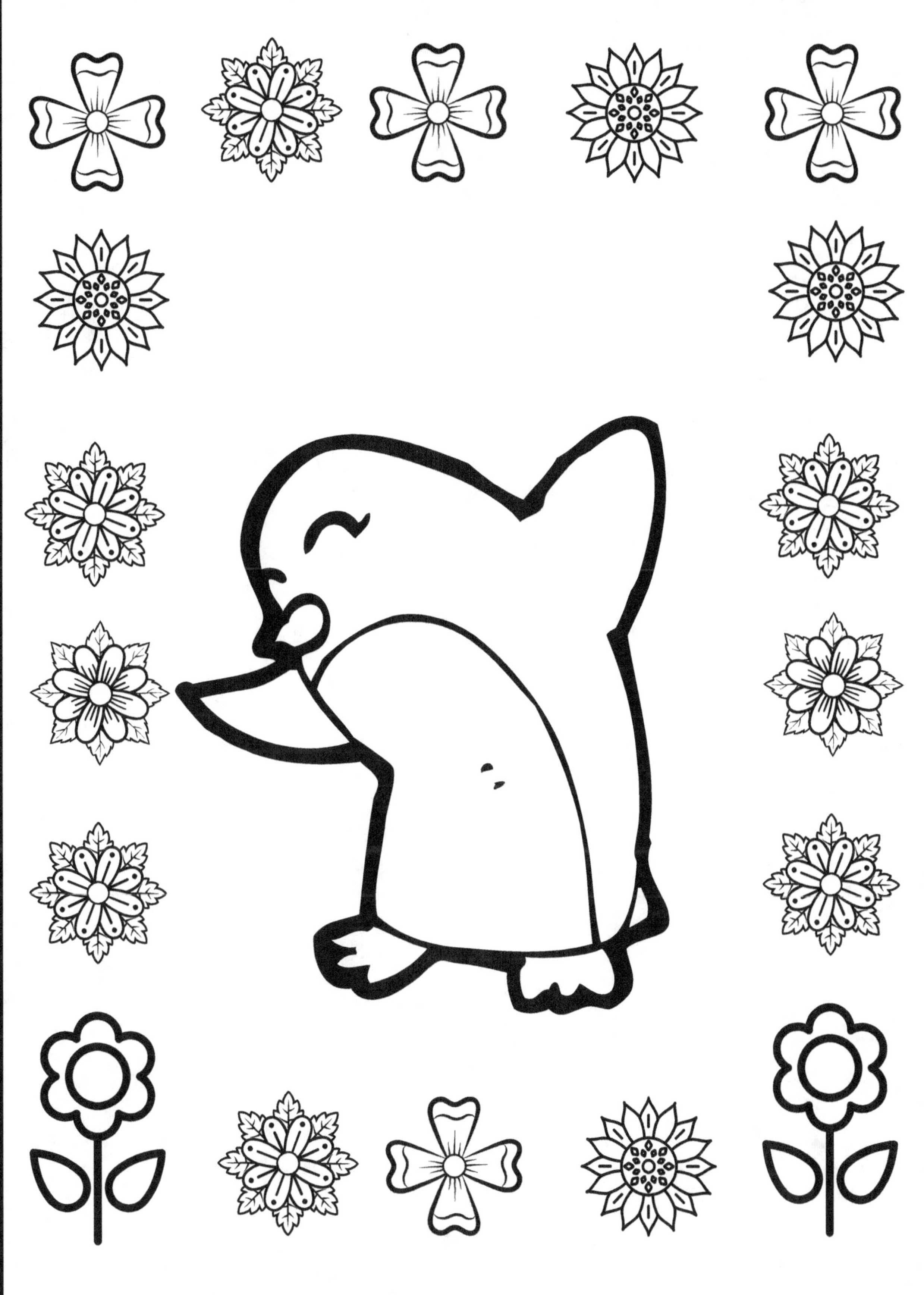

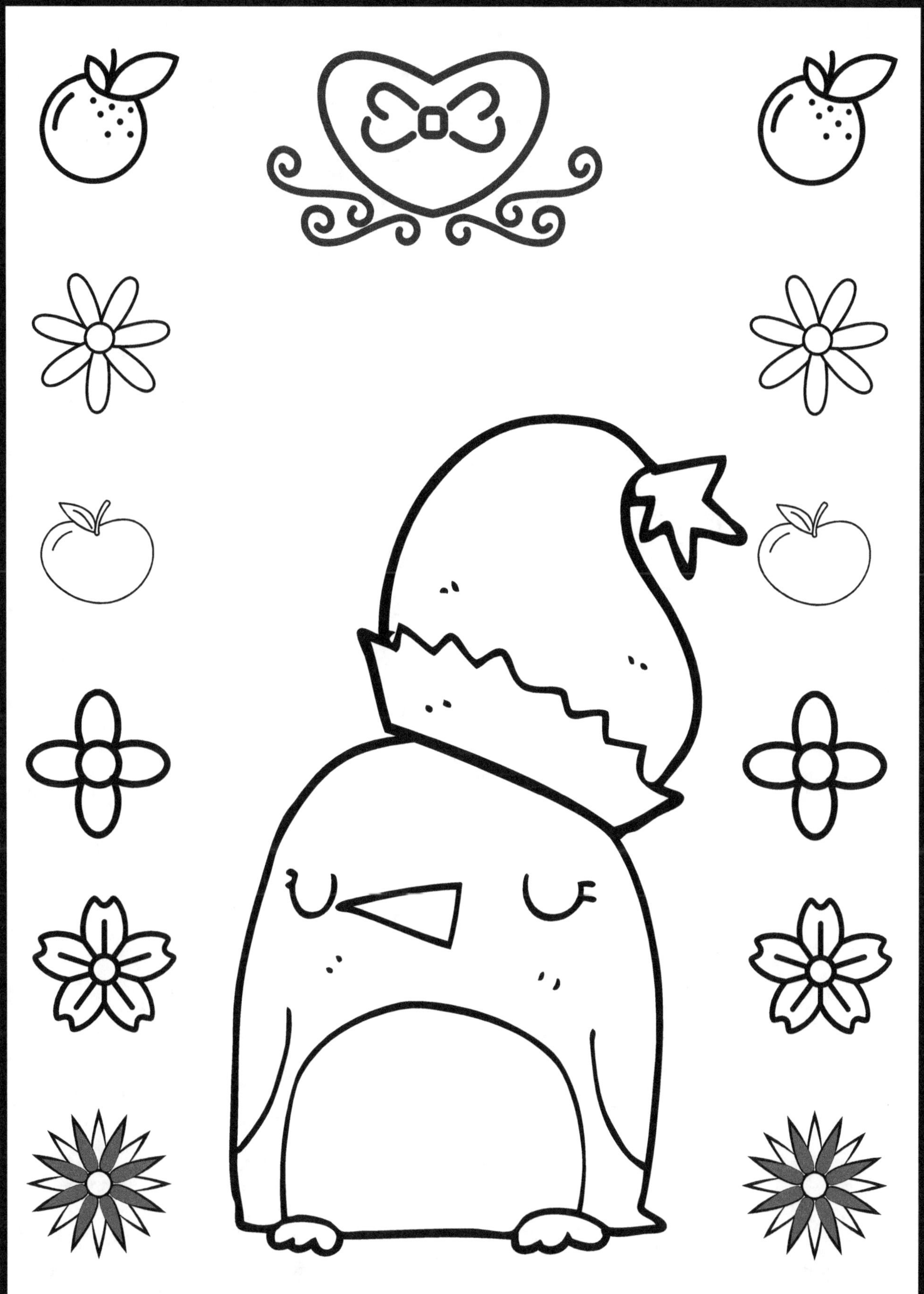